As one of the co-creators of this beautiful anthology, I humbly offer my own personal, sincere acknowledgements and gratitude to four different sets of contributors that have significantly influenced the content of this Speaking From Our Hearts (Volume 1) book.

Firstly to life itself, for giving us all the opportunity to learn, grow and serve; no matter how painful the lessons may have been along the way.

Also, to the amazing co-authors that have had the self-less courage to share their stories, in the hope that invaluable learning may be passed on.

Next, to the truly amazing World Game-Changers community – a growing global movement that is taking action to create a better world.

But most of all to you the reader – for investing in yourself – as you look to embark upon a voyage of new insights and self-discovery…

ISBN 978-1-78222-840-0

Book design, layout and production management by Into Print
www.intoprint.net
+44 (0)1604 832149

Your Change Becomes The World's Change

CHANGE – what an interesting word...but what does it really mean?

Change in a financial sense, when you make a purchase and receive some money back, or change in the sense of making a difference – maybe even both? The latter is exactly the case, as global co-authors, and readers alike, invest in any World Game-Changers (WGC)-related books like this one; knowing that a significant part of their investment is ploughed back to create benefits to many communities.

As an example, World Game-Changers – in partnership with the Growing Trees Network Foundation (Denmark) – has recently (March 2021) taken to planting another Food Forest in Ehimankyene, Ghana; this in conjunction with the 'Grow A Tree Network Ghana'.

World Game-Changers Patron – and Growing Trees Network Foundation Co-Founder and Chairman – Lars Heiselberg Vang Jensen gives some perspective on the vital work of WGC in Ghana...

"Hello Dear World Game-Changers...

The World Game-Changers Food Forest was planted in

Ehimankyene after a supportive heavy rain. Grandpa in the picture (white T-shirt) got emotional, with tears in his eyes. He offered many thanks for the donated trees, saying that the trees give him peace to know that when he dies one day, his family and local people will have something to live from. He insisted to help carry the plants and to plant them; although others respectfully suggested they should do it, because they are younger. He insisted though, to do his part and help.

Due to the generosity of one of WGC's associations, Nottingham Forest Football Club – based in Nottingham, England – many Forest playing kits were sent to Bimbila, Ghana; with the local football team being named The Nyelingbligu Children Football Academy, Bimbilla.

What is happening inside World Game-Changers, is wild and well done. I am proud of all you World Game-Changers, and really admire what is being achieved, and what is unfolding.

WGC makes me smile, reflect, enjoy friendship, grow, feeling supported and awakened – what will and can happen next?

Take care, love and blessings from Denmark..."

Lars

This is how the football kit donation all started. Nottingham Forest Football Club director Jonny Owen (left) hands over one of the shirts to be sent to Ghana, to World Game-Changers director Gary Clarke.

CONTENTS

Introduction

The purpose of this book, as it is with its sister podcast – World Game-Changers – is to share inspirational insights and motivational messages that come from a place of love and compassion, so that people that are looking for positive change in their life, feel inspired to take action.

More specifically, this heart-felt antholgy has been put together with a two-fold purpose in mind. Firstly, to offer real-life stories which serve to hopefully inspire you to want to learn and love more. Secondly – but equally important – is to then have the awareness that you are able to give more, make a difference and leave a positive legacy.

Interesting to hear people's understanding of the word legacy; some are already very clear and driven towards achieving what it means to them; whilst others probably don't even realise they are contributing towards a legacy – in some way – every single day of their lives.

This thought-provoking contrast is encapsulated with a quote from Oprah Winfrey as she turned to her friend & mentor Maya Angelou and stated:

> "I was so proud of myself for building a school for girls in South Africa. That's going to be my greatest legacy – this school." (Winfrey, 2017).

Maya replied with her sage words:

> "You have no idea what your legacy will be; your legacy is every single person who watched your show and said 'I am going to take better care of my health' – every mother who saw a show on abusing children and said 'I will never hit my child again' – to be able to do that, that's your legacy; your legacy is every life you ever touch."

Just as your own understanding of your legacy will be very personal to you, so too will be your individual perception of two other key words in this book – pain and prosperity.

In very simple terms, pain for me, has become a positive lever to gain the awareness to change; whilst prosperity means living a fulfilling life.

We start our journey in Part 1, with my own account – Emerging From The Forest. This lays a foundation for Part 2, as global co-authors share their own compassionate contributions; combining to co-create a rich, diverse mixture of insights and messages.

The third and final part of the book – Hope For A Better Life: Helping You Live In A Better Place – focuses upon some simple steps you can take next to living a fulfilling life; touching upon some key considerations like your purpose, identity, vision and values.

This is part of my legacy – using my experience to be a coach and mentor to others.

Throughout the book, the inspirational chapters are enhanced by simple Words of Wisdom (WOW) along the way...

WOW: You cannot change what you aren't aware of – awareness is a solid foundation for growth

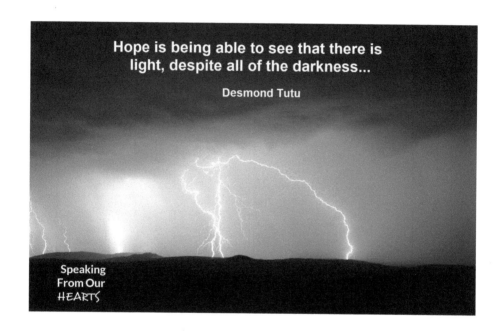

Hope is being able to see that there is light, despite all of the darkness...

Desmond Tutu

Speaking From Our HEARTS

PART ONE:
FROM PAIN TO PURPOSE

Paul D. Lowe

Emerging From The Forest

Although now enjoying a life of prosperity split between the UK and Spain, I spent most of my life living in Nottingham, England – embroiled for decades in an existence of deep-rooted emotional pain and suffering; fuelled by a volatile cocktail of alcohol addiction and violence.

During my colourful journey – dominated by a very black or white polarised approach to life – I had a strong urge to write a book and so in 2000, I self-published a book, called The Game of Life: Half-Time Reflections. This was an autobiographical account of my challenging journey during the first four decades of my life.

Although I now perceive it to have been badly written, people still feedback that it's a 'good book' and well worth the five pounds investment I charged at the time. The cringe-factor has been significantly alleviated though, by the fact it made me three thousand pounds in profit – not bad for someone that took a hopeful punt, and didn't really know what he was doing.

> WOW: Be prepared to try different things – it's amazing what growth there is in embracing something new

As I contemplate the colourful picture my life has unfolded to produce, I believe it has been one heck of a journey. After my parents split up when I was three, my mother and I moved to an inner-city council area called Bestwood Estate to live with my grandmother Winnie. We were soon joined by a beautiful dog called Rocky – boy, how I loved him.

Although we were extremely poor, I often recalled fond memories of those impoverished days, until the age of about seven that is. That's when my mother started seeing a man that lived next door to us, and a year later in 1968, she ended up marrying him.

As much as I vaguely remember the first eight years of my life with pride and happiness – nostalgically reflecting upon a golden era of my passions for music and football – I'm equally polarised in my recollections of how my new step-father's despicable, destructive and depraved behaviour changed my life for the worse.

Initially starting out with random acts of abuse, neglect and mental cruelty towards my mother and me, he then progressed onto consistent spates of sickening violence towards us both; this Beast knew no bounds to his levels of cowardly, grotesque actions.

WOW: Learn to let go of the pain from the past – but not the lessons learnt

As a result of this 'marriage', we uprooted from my beloved Bestwood and moved the other side of Nottingham to the countryside, and for a city boy like me, it was a living hell. All the love and security I had ever known, was removed from my world, leaving me feeling so desperate and sad.

All my certainty had been taken away from me – contact with my grandma Winnie; my passion for listening to music and above all, the dream that maybe one day I would play professional soccer for my hometown team, Nottingham Forest Football Club.

My whole existence had become an unstable mess almost

overnight. The new country-boy kids didn't like football and the Beast deliberately deprived me of these two fervent passions in my life. This acute loss lasted for two long, distressing years until my exile was temporarily over. I can still recall the elation – at the tender age of almost 10 – when my mother told me she was leaving him.

In September 1970, I returned for the final year at my old Junior School and passed my 11+ exam, which gained me a place at the nearby Grammar School. I was now back 'home' and free to enjoy my music and Forest; life was blissfully good once again.

However, this euphoria turned out to be short-lived on several accounts. Firstly, I had begun to feel insecure and depressed because of the cruelty my mother and I had painfully suffered from the Beast; this scarred me more badly than I realized, and the negative legacy was to live on for years.

Secondly, football was banned from being played at Grammar School; it had a steeped tradition of playing rugby and any mention of football was frowned upon by the (mostly) Victorian-style masters presiding over us.

However, if these two aspects were to cause me distress, this was nothing compared to what transpired later. Within a few weeks, my mother was re-united with the Beast and once again, my world was shattered; this marked the start of another three torturous years.

All his previous promises of change and happiness soon disappeared, and the violence and heartlessness soon returned with a vengeance – all this when I was still barely eleven years old. I tried running away from home a couple of times, nervously sleeping rough on the nearby common.

My only salvation through this living hell was the fervent

belief that I would one day be playing for my beloved football club, Forest; but with this obsession being challenged by a new-found coping mechanism – the demon drink!

My mother was a secret drinker and by the age of 12, I was regularly helping myself to tots from her stashes of sherry & whisky – I became addicted!

I was at my breaking point and all my ever-growing instincts for survival were severely being tested to the limit. By now, the cruelty and violence I was experiencing at the hands of the Beast was having a dramatic knock-on effect to me; compounded by witnessing my mother regularly taking beatings from him, too.

A year later in March 1974 – after significant back-to-back defeats for my beloved football team and the realisation that the demon drink was unable to sufficiently numb the effects of my physical, mental & emotional pain – I attempted suicide.

This was one of those 'fight-or-flight' moments, and I made a decision to never fly again! I somehow had the faith to accept there was a reason for this test. If I were experiencing this heart-ache, surely others would be too; and I was prepared to fight for them as well; consciously accepting my life now had purpose.

WOW: A decision to change your life can be made in an instant

Such was my anguish at home that I was now creating a diversionary tactic. I was developing another character, one that would allow me to escape and become somebody else – a facade that was perceived by others as me being a no-non-sense hard-nut – not caring about anyone or anything.

By the time I was barely sixteen, my passion for music was becoming irrelevant, and being replaced by the call to fight for others. This – along with my love for Forest – had given me a strong sense of identity and purpose. My passion towards Forest was beyond most people's comprehension, even many die-hard, Red-shirt supporters.

Looking back, it was a manifestation of an all-or-nothing mindset. There was never any grey in-between. Forest gave me an identity at a time when – through my turbulent childhood – I had effectively lost my own.

> WOW: Your identity is not about your history – it's about what you create for yourself

By now, I also found myself being strongly drawn towards the Irish fraternities, regularly visiting the allotments (caves) of the men-folk on Sunday mornings for a nip or two of Potcheen (home-made Irish potato wine) being mesmerized by tales of bare-knuckle fighting.

Although I was naturally a loving, caring, and sensitive type of child, I had found myself developing a safety mechanism that kept people at arm's length; this front was displayed by being aggressive and confrontational – in effect, I was living a massive lie!

Consequently in November 1974, things were about to come to a head and change forever; after being kept behind at school for a detention, I knew that returning home late that afternoon would mean big trouble. I began trembling with anticipation as I sprinted home with all the adrenaline and nervous energy of a hunted gazelle. As I entered the back door, the inevitable happened; the Beast attacked me incessantly. I somehow weathered the onslaught and wiped the streams of crimson blood from my face. As I did so, I managed to catch sight of a bread knife on the kitchen table; I lunged for it and took my stance with only one thought in mind, and it wasn't to cut bread! The hunted had now become the hunter – my temper was so fierce, like a caged and tormented tiger.

The winds of change were now blowing, and this was the first time I became conscious of my ability to take back control of my life away from the Beast. Like all bullies when threatened with their own treatment, he cowered away.

The anticipated sequel having not materialized, my mother and I simply packed our bags and left with me quietly and vowing to the Beast that one day I would return and get my revenge.

This proved to be a significant turning point in my life; because of all the emotional pain I had suffered over the previous few years, I now found myself more than ever becoming alcohol dependent; whilst at the same time, becoming embroiled in constant conflicts and physical fights.

As I progressed beyond my teens, one of the lowest points of my life occurred on New Year's Eve 1982, with the news that my Grandma Winnie had died. As an 'old-school' matriarch, she was so resilient, strong, and was as solid and tough as a majestic oak tree.

After Winnie's death, to say I waged war on society would be a massive understatement. I took it upon myself to be judge, jury, and executioner towards any Tom, Dick, or Harry that I perceived was a bully; I was now a rebel with a cause!

For a while, sheer willpower and determination saw me turn things around. At the age of 23, I got married and by 27, had two beautiful children and a third on the way. However the cracks re-appeared as I'd never managed to consistently curb my drinking – the demon drink had me in its vice-like clutches.

In June 1988, some 14 years on, I reached rock-bottom in my life; I split up from my wife and kids and began to drift into complete oblivion. Like all heavy drinkers, my thought processes had become badly distorted and I couldn't rid myself of the memories relating to the previous torture and abuse.

It was at this point, that I finally confronted the Beast; those years of hatred had been allowed to fester and in my emotionally-twisted logic, it was now time to re-dress the balance for all the anguish and pain he had caused. I had constantly re-lived every slap, punch, and sadistic act he had previously delivered to my mother and me.

The upshot was I intended to kill him, but after setting about my 'duty', the Universe intervened and my intention was not fulfilled, with both our lives being spared – his from death and mine from serving a life sentence in prison.

> WOW: Learn to control your thoughts – or else they'll control you

Coming so close to totally ruining my life instigated another 'dry-run.' I was re-united with my family, and set out on another hopeful path. I got a good job and once again, was starting to do what I had long-since been conscious of being put on this earth to do – help others.

Part of that helping, included raising significant funds for many charitable causes. However, my well-intentioned fund-raising exploits would always be tested by heavy drinking binges.

Subsequently becoming unemployed in 1991, I decided to embark upon a long phase of learning – spanning over a decade – that resulted in me achieving a teaching degree and a Master's degree, with my studies fitting-in around disciplined periods of abstinence from destructive drinking binges.

More important than the academic achievement though, was

the process of continuous improvement I resonated with. This philosophy was instrumental in laying the foundations for my personal development journey; I was greatly inspired by the prospect of being the best I could be and then, serving others.

> WOW: The greatest investment you can make is in yourself. If you don't believe in YOU, how will anyone else?

Whilst this was an admirable focus, I was still dealing with my own destructive demons. My views were still very polarized – life was either black or white, and I rarely showed any flexibility, especially in matters of potential conflict, where I would be judge, jury, and executioner – then ask questions later!

Irrespective, I look back over the decades and reflect on what lessons I have learnt and how these can be passed-on for the benefit of others. Lessons – not in an academic sense – but in a real practical life-improving way. Put simply, I don't want people to learn the hard way, like I did.

The breakthrough in my constant progress-sabotage cycle appeared after an almighty binge-drinking session. On February 7th February 2010, I barely awoke from a drunken stupor with the realization I was going to die – I believed and felt my time had come!

Throughout the following critical days, I somehow mustered the awareness to know that life would be very different if I survived; obviously I did and to this day, I haven't touched a drop of alcohol since.

My mind sometimes used to meander down memory lane and take me back to one of my founding beliefs that the only way out of the hard-fought days in Bestwood, would be sport or education.

After spending so many years on believing sport was the

answer, it's ironic how education and learning has proved to be my salvation. A by-product of my early education path was to pen a poem about the demon drink – called…

A Question of Bottle

A man in his prison cell, all alone and he's down;

His eyes are all bloodshot and his face wears a frown

One way or another, a life behind bars;

He once had it all, fast money – fast cars

But now he is broken, and everything is lost;

The legacy of booze, was it all worth the cost?

He needed his tipple to help him get by;

Now everything's gone, he wished he'd stayed dry

The drink was a comfort when things got too tough;

At night he felt numb, in the morning just rough

The lies and the violence he promised would cease;

But booze had control and never gave peace

Tears stroke his cheeks as he thinks of it now;

Perhaps he would change, if only he knew how?

It's a question of bottle and which one to choose;

The one full of love or the one full of booze

Neither is easy and both promise gains;

But one offers hope – the other just pains

So when you're alone with only booze as your friend;

Reach out for support – it's easier in the end.

Even in my darkest hours, I had a sense of purpose albeit vague, that has continued to grow over the decades. Today, my awareness manifests itself in the work I do both as a coach and mentor, and also through the charity & community projects I'm involved in – embracing my identity as:

Developing World Game-Changers.

All my life, I've always committed to making a positive difference in others' lives; none more so since the formation of the World Game-Changers movement – planting the seeds for change throughout worldwide communities.

I now recognize that all those years in the 'dark soil' were merely a planting exercise, for when the environmental conditions were right, and this particular acorn would be ready to transform into a thriving oak tree – making significant contributions to life's universal forests.

I stopped living a lie and reclaimed my true identity of being a loving, caring, and sensitive soul. I have come to understand the importance of love – of self & others – as the emotional water in the aridity of life's deserts. I know the benefits and positive impact of constantly striving to meet your needs for growth and contribution.

Imagine if you can, what life would have been like if the pieces of my jigsaw had been different and contributed towards creating a completely different picture of my life. Can you imagine what life would have been like if my mother hadn't married the Beast in August 1968 and as a result, I wouldn't have endured long-term pain & suffering – forging my vision to leave the world a better place? Also, what life might have been like if:

❖ I hadn't made that suicidal fight-or-flight decision in March 1974 – vowing to never fly again or become a victim – and that I would commit to a lifetime journey of **Learning**?

❖ In September 1991 – I hadn't made the decision to take another significant step on my learning voyage, discovering self-awareness and the importance of relationships and **Loving**?

❖ In October 2010, I hadn't formed the Sporting HEARTS charity and a decade later, World Game-Changers, positively affecting thousands of people's lives – contributing to leave a global **Legacy**?

Although the past cannot be changed, it will contain some very colourful pieces that can be used to create a new, empowering picture for your life – something that emerged as a result of creating my 'Three Pillars of Life' approach.

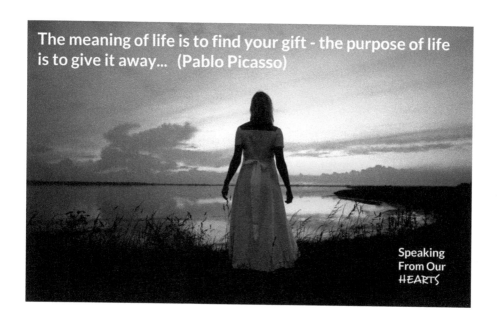

The meaning of life is to find your gift - the purpose of life is to give it away... (Pablo Picasso)

Speaking From Our HEARTS

WOW: Leave your legacy in people's hearts – then it's indelible

PART TWO:
INSPIRING STORIES OF TRANSFORMATION

Aimée Mosco (USA)

Faith Is The Mother Of Hope

I woke up gasping for breath. It was still dark. I'd had a horrible dream that I was standing on a hill overlooking a valley which lay under a pile of rubble. As I looked down on the valley, I knew that people were trapped, or worse, under the boulders that were shaken loose by the burst of energy that rocked the Earth. The air was cloudy with reddish dust and the ground was cracked deeply in all directions. I felt despair in my body. Through my tears I kept repeating the words, "There's nothing left. There's nothing left."

I couldn't breathe when I opened my eyes. It felt like there was a thousand-pound weight sitting on my chest. My heart was pounding like a bass drum and I couldn't speak but a mumble to call for help.

Not again.

My mother came rushing into my room with a flashlight in her hand. She tilted my head back and put her face close to my mouth to see if I was still breathing. She pulled my eyelids back and begged me to stay with her. She yelled to my father, "Her lips are blue. Pull the car out."

She wrapped me in a blanket and lifted my limp body out of my sweat-soaked bed. She was being careful, but she was moving with haste. She loaded me into the car, and we were off to the emergency room. Again.

I don't remember my thoughts on that particular trip to the hospital. I may have passed out from the lack of oxygen, or I may just have tucked those thoughts away in the archives of my mind as a preservation tactic. I don't know. I remember well what happened when we got to the hospital though. Those memories have flooded my mind at the most unlikely times throughout my life.

After we got to the hospital, there was a flurry of activity around me. I was poked with needles, prodded, shaken, and stirred. I was medicated and admitted, then deposited in the room right next to the nurses' station of the pediatric section in our small-town hospital. Again.

I remember being acutely aware of my surroundings as I was delivered to my room away from home. I noticed that the walls were painted mint green. I remember the expression on my nurse's face as she raised the head of the bed behind me and pulled a loose-knit blanket up to my waist. It was one of pity mixed with compassion. I watched her face disappear as she rolled the sides of the thick plastic oxygen tent down around me so I could no longer see her features clearly. I heard the ice cubes cracking against one another as she poured them into the oxygen maker. I felt the cool mist fill the tent as I sunk into sadness and isolation. Again.

The whole time my mother stood watch next to my bed as my guardian angel in the flesh. She always stayed with me as long as she could. I knew, though, that she would have to leave me at some point. I watched her movements like a hawk so I could prepare myself for that dreaded moment when she had to go.

When the oxygen tent was running smoothly and the activity died down in the room, she turned the lights down low and sat beside my bed in a chair for a while. I was exhausted and it was hard to talk, so I just laid there fighting to breathe. Then I saw my mother reach into her purse. She pulled out a blue leather glasses case with little colored flowers stamped into it. There was a shiny gold clasp at the top. She slid her hand under the tent to give me her glasses case. I had always loved that case. I saw my mother take it out of her purse a hundred times. It always caught my eye because I thought it was so pretty.

She told me that she had to go home, but if I took her glasses case, then she would have to come back in the morning to get it. It was twisted logic, but it made sense in my four-year-old mind. She certainly wouldn't leave an important piece of equipment and not come back to get it, would she? No, she wouldn't.

Even though it was just a glasses case, it meant something so much more to me. It was a special piece of my mother that she offered to me in exchange for my faith. I will never forget the case or that moment as long as I live because it served as a light for me to connect with hope in the darkness of the moment.

I'm not convinced I would have made it through the night had my mother not shown me the light. I held onto that case for dear life that night. It meant to me that my mother was coming back and that I had to stay alive to give it back to her.

This harrowing routine was something my mother and I played out too many times from 1973 to 1978. Twenty-four times over those 5 years to be exact.

I was born a month early. I wasn't considered premature but given that the lungs are the last of the organs to develop, it seems that I wasn't quite cooked when I arrived in this world. My lungs were weak and susceptible. They always took the hit when the weather turned damp, or a bug was going around. Something that was a minor irritation to one of my peers turned into full-blown pneumonia for me, and a whole lot of heartache for my Mom.

Gasping for breath, trips to the hospital, chest x-rays, and oxygen tents became the norm for me in those early years. Even though I was little, I was very much aware that I walked a thin line between life and death. My tomorrows were not a given. In fact, I assumed on many occasions that I would die because the sickness felt like a monster that had me in its grip. The fight made me so tired. I didn't want to give up but in the darkest hours, hope felt out of reach and death a certainty.

My mother, true to her word, came back to reunite with her glasses case and keep vigil again by my side. I felt elated when I saw a distorted view of her through the plastic tent surrounding me. She walked through the doorway of my room and it was like the sun began to shine again just for me. The darkness of my hospital room nearly swallowed me up during the night as I clutched the case.

My mother sat next to my bed with her knitting all day long while I floated in and out of sleep. She only left my side for a few minutes at a time. She told me stories and talked to me when I was awake, she explained to me what was happening when I was

18

carted off to have another x-ray, or when I was being given another shot. She made it all seem like it was going to be ok even though in those moments, it was not.

When the sun started to go down and shadows appeared in my room, the dread began to set in. I knew my mother would have to leave me again. I felt the tears well up when I saw her gathering her things. My chest tightened even more. I was afraid to navigate the darkness on my own.

My mother lifted the side of the oxygen tent up to place her glasses case in my hand again, reminding me that she was leaving a little piece of herself with me until her return in the morning. The tears broke loose and fell down my cheeks. I didn't want her to go but I didn't have the strength to protest. All I could do was cry.

As she walked out the door, I clutched the glasses case and pictured her face in my mind. I imagined that the glasses case was her hand. I kept my eyes closed so I could trick myself into believing it was her hand that I was clutching.

I fell asleep, glued to the glasses case and holding on to that image, having complete faith that she would come back.

She came back the next morning, and every other morning when I woke up in a hospital bed. She always left me with some glimmer of hope the night before when it was time to go. She pulled something of meaning out of her purse or her knitting bag, placed it in my hand and reminded me that she would be back.

It always worked. Whatever she handed me with her imprint on it, strengthened my faith in a new tomorrow. I came to believe that the morning would bring with it light, not just from the sun, but the kind of light that illuminates the space which holds darkness, fear, and despair on the inside.

My mother acted on instinct fueled by love, and whether she realized it or not at the time, she gave me one of the greatest gifts a person can give to another. She taught me how to hold hands with hope through faith and how to always find a light in a dark space. While those were hard years with so much uncertainty that left an indelible imprint on my soul, I wouldn't trade them for anything.

I grew to be fearless and determined. I lived life to the fullest as my lungs became stronger. The faith that carried me through those hard times was what allowed me to have hope for something better with each new day. I wasted no opportunity to experience the 'better'. I took dance lessons, gymnastics, I ran track, I was a cheerleader, I played softball and baseball (as a solo girl on a boys' team), took music lessons, camped, became a life-guard, I sang, and I joined every club I could in-between. The rest of my childhood became a colorful collage of better days.

As the end of an era approached, I had to decide where I would go for college. I had learned well how to overcome fear, so it didn't register as I made my choice. I chose to move across the country and away from everything and everyone I knew. I felt no fear, only hope for what was yet to come. My friends and family protested, but I was determined. I knew I would be ok.

The first few weeks of college tested my faith. I was so home-sick and uncertain. I wondered if I had made the right decision. I wondered if my friends and family had been right. If I should have stayed closer to home. As I lay on my dorm room bed one day after class, contemplating, I looked around the room and felt tears well up. Why was I crying? I couldn't actually remember the last time I had cried.

Then it struck me. The walls in my dorm room were the same color as the walls in that hospital room where I had spent so much time. Mint green. All the feelings came flooding back to me in that moment as I realized the stars had aligned for me to be in a setting that would bring me back to center and give me the opportunity reconnect with faith and hope as I began the next chapter of my life.

My tears slowly stopped falling and sadness turned to laughter. I laughed out loud and made a plan with hope at the helm! The next week I arranged to move into a new dorm room with blue walls. When I moved into my new room, I put fear and uncertainty in a locked box on my bookshelf just as I had learned to do all those years ago. I invited my old best friend and silent roommate, hope, to share the space with me instead.

Hope and I went on to travel the world together. We held hands through marriage, childbirth, divorce, marriage again. She was my shoulder when my nest became empty. She was my ever-present light when darkness rolled in, and my encouragement to keep going. Never has a friend been so true. I will forever be grateful for our relationship, and for the introduction by faith, from which my hope was born.

Bill & Jenni Burridge (South Africa)

From Bridges & Ballet To Butterflies

"So, how do I look?" I asked Dave, my best mate and fellow engineering student at the university of Cape Town.

"Like a right tart" he smirked.

"OK, give me another swig of that beer and let's go do this thing" I responded, faking courage.

We were headed to a Rocky Horror Show themed party at the neighbouring ladies residence. Dave's new partner, Gail, had pressed him to bring me along as a blind date for her friend and roommate, Jenni.

Picture the scene… beer-swilling engineering student in full cross-dress with borrowed stockings and skimpy lace underwear, attempting to impersonate Frank N. Furter.

As I think back to that defining moment in my life, I shake my head and laugh at my blissful ignorance of the Universe's unfolding plan…

I was about to meet the love of my life to be. What a first impression!

Mercifully, Jenni was blessed with a great sense of humour and our relationship continued, even after the 'rocky' start.

Amongst our peers in the engineering faculty, word spread quickly that Dave and I were dating students from the university's ballet school. Publicly, we revelled in the boost to our 'cool street cred'.

Privately, however, we soon began to lament how underequipped our calculator-and-logic type personalities were to deal with the emotional tempestuousness of our artistic-and-creative natured girlfriends!

On reflection, Jenni and I have been married longer than Britney Spears has been alive – we may, ironically, have stumbled upon the secret to relationship longevity.

If you ever experimented with magnets and iron filings in a

school science class, you'll appreciate the saying: 'unlike poles attract'. Well, 'unlike poles', Jenni and I most certainly were!

Post-university our relationship was soon put to the test.

While I joined a major construction company specialising in bridge building and moved across the country, Jenni accepted an offer to run a dance school for kids and took off for the beautiful Indian Ocean island of Mauritius.

After a year apart, I flew out – excited to join Jenni on a three-week holiday only to discover that she had begun to succumb to the charms of a softly-spoken local man with an intoxicatingly romantic French accent.

It was clearly an unfair competition and I had to act quickly; on the eve of Christmas at that symbolic turning point – sunset – I proposed.

Mother Nature though, was not impressed. Within days, she unleashed upon us the wrath of Claudette – one of the most devastating weather cyclones to make landfall in Mauritius in fifteen years.

Claudette's destructive force pummelled our breezy vacation let throughout the night, scaring the living hell out of both of us. But despite her best efforts to disrupt our relationship, the experience served to strengthen our bond.

In Cape Town, South Africa a little more than a year later, we were married.

After the wedding we moved to a beautiful little town on the south coast of Natal where I got absorbed into the testosterone-fuelled culture of a large bridge construction team. Jenni on the other hand, bought and operated a health and fitness studio, exclusively for ladies.

At home, we struggled to reconcile our different outlooks. Jenni's love of form clashed with my obsession with function. The temporary nature of construction projects led me to view spends on curtains, carpets and the like as wasteful.

Instead I believed in spending only on essentials… like a belter of a hi-fi stereo system! At least when time allowed us, we could party like there was no tomorrow.

As time wore on, though, I became increasingly unsettled about living in a permanent state of transition and wanted something different.

When I chose to study engineering I knew deep down that it would be an imperfect fit.

In wanting to 'do the right thing', I had suppressed my inner-voice and allowed myself to be guided by peer pressure and the advice of others. Now my inner-voice began to speak up.

I reflected that whereas my working life had always revolved around things, my heart desired to experience working with something infinitely more challenging and exciting – people.

The defining moment came in the midst of a torrential down-pour, late at night out on site. I decided it was time for a change. I left my job in construction and headed back to the University of Cape Town to embark on a year of intensive full-time study towards an MBA degree.

Jenni found an hourly-paid job as an aerobics instructress, running up to five high-intensity classes a day just to take care of our living expenses. It was exhausting work for her but, my goodness, she was fit!

The year flashed past and after graduating, I joined a huge multi-national, in the sales and marketing division. Loving the change, I eagerly looked forward to realising my passion for working with, motivating and directing people.

Life was good and, not wanting to mess with that, I easily suppressed any ideas of starting a family. That is, until the tenth anniversary of our marriage.

On that red letter day, Jenni pronounced, with uncharacteristic forcefulness approaching that of cyclone Claudette, that the time to start a family had finally arrived and further delay was not an option. I had no choice but to do the honourable thing.

Our beautiful baby Bianca was born in Cambridge during a short work assignment to the UK. Some four years later, back in Cape Town, our wonderful son Casey arrived to complete our much desired 'pigeon pair'.

However, I had precious little time for playing happy families over the next ten years, with my focus on climbing the corporate ladder. To enhance my CV I took on various roles in distribution, project management and technology.

My work ethic was noticed, and I landed an expatriate assignment to the corporate headquarters in London. Our family association with England, where I was also born and raised as a child, was about to be renewed.

We lived very comfortably and wanted for absolutely nothing… except that increasingly elusive commodity – family time together.

My new programme management role had me shuttling – at one stage weekly – between London and the US, where we were piloting the development of a web-based software solution for international roll-out.

It was a challenging and exhausting time for me. For Jenni it meant devoting herself to the kids and, on weekends, picking up the pieces of a frequently shattered husband.

The aftermath of the dot-com collapse caused the members of our project steering board to grow increasingly cautious and, after eighteen months – and despite solid progress with the pilot project – they pulled the rug on the programme… and with it, my job!

Fortunately, as that door closed another opened. I was assigned a senior management role, in IT. Though hugely thankful for the lifeline, I was inwardly disconcerted. My career path had U-turned away from my passion – working with people. The steel and concrete of my past had been replaced by 'bits and bytes'.

At about that time my company flip-flopped in its policy towards leadership development. Functional specialists, previously disadvantaged in selection for leadership positions, would now be favoured over 'all-rounders'. In other words, deep expertise in one field would be preferred to broad exposure in numerous fields.

It hit me like a ton of bricks. For twenty years I had sweated to gain the wide exposure seen as crucial for advancement, only to find that the game had changed.

I learnt a salutary lesson. It was finally time to start playing my own 'game', doing what I loved rather than what I thought was expected of me. That change of heart soon attracted an exciting new opportunity.

The IT division embraced a radical cost-reduction programme that necessitated the appointment of an internal communications manager to help build trust and two-way engagement between leadership and the employees. In simple terms this was a role that involved working with and inspiring people.

I jumped at the chance to apply, relying on pure passion – and a little help from the Universe – to land the job. Having the courage to follow my heart felt exciting, invigorating and liberating.

Over the next three years I became totally immersed in my great new job and was soon asked to join the corporate communications team and manage internal communications for the entire organisation.

Despite exciting developments on the work front, my life transformation was still far from complete, with the 'holy grail' of quality family time beyond my grasp. It was time for another curve ball from the Universe!

With my assignment drawing to a close, my thoughts turned to the future. With a major restructuring of the subsidiary, job prospects at home looked bleak, so I enquired about the chances of permanent employment in the UK.

To my great relief, I received a very positive response. Eager to share the good news with Jenni, I left work early, for once. Jenni's reaction to my news, though, was as shocking as it was straightforward.

"Six years is long enough, Bill. It's time for the family to go home (to South Africa). My mind is made up. Now you must decide if you want to join us."

I had clearly failed to 'read the tealeaves' while living in my work bubble. Realising that time had just been called on my career as I knew it, a feeling of anxiety, uncertainty and even resentment washed over me.

The Universe knew differently.

Up until then, I had been financially supporting a close relative that had fallen on hard times. In her wisdom, seeing little improvement in the situation, Jenni suggested channelling our support into hiring a life coach.

'Great idea' I thought to myself, 'but what on earth is a life coach?' Embarrassed with myself, I turned to Google.

To cut a very long story short, my research culminated in a very helpful meeting with Neil, the owner of a life coach training company and a man with whom I enjoyed instant rapport.

As I looked to close the conversation by thanking him for his advice, he surprised me by turning his attention firmly to me: "Bill, it's clear you're facing a great deal of change on a number of fronts in your life. I strongly recommend that you give life coaching a try for yourself."

Neil insisted on connecting me with Sharon, a young Manchester-based life coach who had graduated from his training programme. With more than a little scepticism, I agreed to a series of telephone coaching sessions with her.

To my great surprise – to Neil's and Sharon's eternal credit – I was blown away by the sheer power and simplicity of the coaching programme she so skilfully guided me through.

Shaking with excitement, I called Neil and got straight to the point:

"I absolutely love life coaching. It's simple, it works and it's life-changing. I'd love to introduce this training in South Africa – how about it?"

We concluded a deal, and in due course, Neil and his lovely wife Natasha flew to South Africa to help with the start up my new company, New Insights Africa.

Neil and Natasha quickly identified in Jenni a natural coaching ability and passion and Natasha channelled a lot of effort into coaching Jenni in the application of their life coaching system.

In the space of just a few months Jenni and I went from being ships in the night – sacrificing quality time together for the trappings of my corporate career – to being jointly involved in our own successful life coach training business.

Today I'm privileged to own New Insights, both in South Africa and the UK. Whereas I run the business and training side, Jenni provides coaching services to trainee coaches. As you might expect, we bring very different yet complementary skills and perspectives to the business table.

A few years ago, I felt the time was right to do something I had long dreamed of doing...I wrote and published a book.

It wasn't about building bridges (of the concrete sort), succeeding in corporate life or even starting a small business. I wrote about awakening to the magic of the life you love – a personal development book based on my journey to find and live my life purpose.

The cover page of the quirkily titled 'A Boerewors Roll for the Soul', (boerewors is a type of South African traditional sausage) features a little creature that Jenni long ago adopted as a symbol of her own spirituality... the humble, yet exquisite butterfly.

It symbolises my deep thanks and appreciation to Jenni for the role she played in my transformation, and our coming together.

Jenni's Perspective:

From Human Doings To Human Beings!

'When you know better, you do better'
(Oprah Winfrey)

I don't think there is anyone, who at some point in his or her life hasn't said: 'I wish I had known then, what I know now!'

I've said this many times, but I know now that this wish is not my wish, because, if I had known, I would never have embarked on this amazing journey of self-realisation and evolving consciousness.

I believe that managing the energy of thought, perception and the linked emotions, is the key to a fulfilled and happy life. When you truly understand that your 'doing' is a direct result of your thoughts and emotions, only then can you take full responsibility for your life experiences.

And then it comes to 'being'. I finally learnt that Love, Joy, Peace and Happiness, are states of being that you can CHOOSE. The choice comes with a consciousness whilst IN the present moment, and the awareness OF the moment, and the thoughts you hold ABOUT the moment!

It all makes perfect sense, and the processes are so simple and very empowering. Yet you get so busy with life, and ego-jostling, and wanting to be 'right', that you forget who you are at the deepest level.

This wasn't clear to Bill and me in those early days. We used to argue and fight about 'reality'! I 'had my head in the clouds', and 'needed to get down to earth, and he 'just didn't get it!' Of course I was going to expect miracles, who wouldn't?

And here, the fire and water signs made… steam!

Bill and I and our children, have had many memorable experiences together – some fabulous and some not so much. However, each experience contained within it a lesson and an opportunity to learn and grow, but only as long as we were prepared to do the work.

One particularly significant experience was our time spent in England. We embarked on an adventure that was to last six years – three years longer than originally planned. It was exciting, with so many new things to discover.

A new country, a new home and wonderful travel opportunities which took us to France, Spain, Greece, Antigua, Tobago and the Maldives. We lived more than comfortably. The kids were enrolled at a wonderful school; we had everything we wanted, and almost everything we needed.

What was missing was a wholesome family life. Bill's corporate career out-paced my life with the children and, as he has said, we were 'ships passing in the night' with very little time together.

There were days when I felt filled with gratitude for the beautiful English countryside, for our magnificent manor house and exquisite garden with roses, daffodils, ponds and ducks – and then there were days when the loneliness caught up with me, and I ached for the familiarity and rhythm of Africa.

I was stuck, facing a conundrum! In England I had everything I needed in the world of form. Yet spiritually, I felt incomplete and my need for love and connection was not being met.

I tried really hard to keep afloat and grateful, putting my everything into the children, so that they felt whole while their father was absent.

I knew that this life of imbalance was not sustainable. It was especially obvious at bedtime when Bianca and Casey longed for Bill to read them stories and kiss them goodnight.

I yearned to run barefoot on African soil again. I got to a point, where I was more than happy to give up all the 'stuff' in order to live according to my highest values of balance and family.

And, so, after much ado, we returned to Cape Town. Bill has described the sequence of events leading up to his life-changing, massive leap, from corporate life to running life coach training companies in South Africa and the UK.

And here we are!

Bill runs the business using his people, communication and marketing skills, brilliantly – and I am now a life coach.

I call my practice 'True Essence Coaching'. It's my mission to help my clients find THEIR true essence, as I have, in order to live authentically and consciously. My inner and outer Purposes are finally aligned!

Bill and I will never be the same, and we don't want to be the same, but where we are now is getting into step on the Path of Life!

WOW: Joy is the result of a coming together of heart and mind

https://www.life-coach-training-uk.com

Kevin Searcey (UK)

Who Am I?

I was born in the early 1960's in a rough – but tightly-knit – part of Nottingham, known as St. Anns. Although times were hard and the family were poor, this was only in a financial sense. I enjoyed a loving, secure childhood; one that contributed towards giving me the confidence to progress to a high level in karate and subsequently engage in many fight tournaments.

I suppose 'Who am I?' is one of those questions – along with 'what's the meaning of life?' – that everyone asks themselves from time to time. I know this is something that has generally floated through my mind over the last 25 years or so.

Having been married for 10 years, I then found myself off work after severely damaging my right knee in a karate accident in 1993. As a result, money was very scarce and – after many heated arguments – my wife (Janet) and I eventually spilt up in 1994.

It was devastating for me to leave my two kids – Paul and Kaylee behind. Soon after, I learnt that Janet was expecting our third child; Nicola being born in November 1994.

All I had in the world was a few clothes and a battered Robin Reliant Estate car; the guy I purchased it off used to race Reliants at stock car events and told me how fast it was. I found this to be true, one day coming back to Nottingham from Sheffield – being stopped by the police for doing 90 mph!

Now separated from my ex-wife, I moved back in with my loving parents; they were extremely supportive and gave me food & shelter. I suppose this is the first time I became conscious of my identity question – who am I? – because I had gone from a proud family man providing for his loved ones, to someone that now needed his parents' support.

The ensuing months were painful in every imaginable way. Physically, I had to cope with knee operations and rehab; but this physical pain was absolutely nothing compared to the emotional suffering I was experiencing – due to missing my children, whom I adored.

Nothing seemed to go right; I was now fighting for custody to get to see my children and I remember thinking daily, 'when was this ever going to end?'.

Missing my kids was made even harder by the fact I knew how much they missed me too. The arguments carried on and my kids seemed to be in the middle of it all. Eventually my ex-wife allowed my children to come and see me at my parents' home.

I have priceless memories of sitting there on a Saturday morning – watching 'Saved By The Bell' and 'Rugrats' – with me in the middle of all of us, eating grandma's special toasties.

In May, it was my birthday, and I got some money off my family; all I could think of was using the cash to treat my kids to a McDonalds. The year rolled by and the visits to the solicitors seemed never-ending.

As 1994 was drawing to a close, and I couldn't get the thought of having no money, out of my head; I was determined to look after my kids for Christmas, so I reluctantly sold my beloved Reliant Robin.

January 1995 rapidly introduced itself and I painfully recall wondering what this year would have in store for me? By now, I'm feeling sorry for myself and completely in victim mode; I had a knee that kept giving way, so had to wear a leg brace until the reconstruction later that year.

My mind had become one messy myriad of negative, ego-driven self-doubting thoughts; I really could not see a future and anyway, what good would I be to my wonderful children? They deserve a better dad than I could ever be.

The 9th March 1995 was a very significant date – other than my lovely Mum's birthday – because this was the day I thought I'd met my soul-mate Lorraine. I woke that day to the sun shining into my eyes through a gap in the blinds, and wondering what was in store for me today.

I dragged myself out of bed that morning and duly wished my

adoring mother a happy birthday. I was supposed to be going out that night – with my friend Adrian – but I asked Mum if she'd phone him and relay that I couldn't make it because I was ill.

Mum guessed what was really wrong with me; I was skint but too proud to say; she gave me a tenner and would not take it back. She insisted she just wanted to see me happy and to go out and have a good time. Reluctantly, I rang Adrian to say I would go out later.

Later that evening we turned up at a place called Turners – a little club above the local Mapperley Co-op store. We stood at the bar chatting away and Adrian seemed to be pre-occupied with looking at some ladies; commenting how pretty they were.

To be honest I remember not being interested; or maybe I was just plain scared, as I did not want to get hurt again?

I felt like a fish out of water I stood there at the bar sipping my pint and trying to look confident, while Adrian talked to the ladies. I glanced over at the dance floor and noticed a blonde woman who intrigued me; she was full of life and had a cocky walk. She seemed full of confidence when she walked to her friends near me at the bar.

The night was over and – as Adrian and me walked towards the exit – a bizarre thing happened… I felt something or someone turn me around, but no one was there (to this day I still find this amazing and believe a spiritual presence was there to guide me).

Then we were suddenly ushered out the club and I thought I had lost the blonde; my heart sank, but as I walked out I heard a voice shout…

"See you next week" it was the cheeky confident blonde.

I could not wait for next week and could not get blondie out of my head. The following week, I turned up again with my friend Adrian, but she was not there. I don't think I took my eyes off the door that night.

I had just about given up, but then in the middle of the dance floor, I saw blondie and my heart skipped a beat as she came over to say 'hello' again.

After eventually establishing her name was Lorraine – and swapping phone numbers – my world was then significantly challenged when she announced she was married. Nonetheless, we became friends over the ensuing months, and I loved seeing her, even if things were strictly plutonic.

In May of 1995, I got a letter from a housing association, offering me a one-bedroom flat. At last, some good news! A couple of weeks later – with loads of support from my loving family, I moved into my new abode; although I still felt isolated.

Undeterred, I saved every penny I could – even letting the electricity run out – so I would have enough money for when my kids came to visit; as well as having sufficient to go to Turners night club.

I carried on going up to Turners, but didn't see Lorraine for weeks; then one day, she turned up and seemed very low. She told me she had split up with her husband and was living in a refuge; I responded by telling her I had a flat and she was welcome to visit anytime she wanted.

Over the next few weeks, we found that we were falling in love and eventually shared a loving kiss; then Lorraine pulled back and quickly left. Confused and hurt, I sat on my little step outside my flat – watching every car that passed, hoping it was her.

The anticipated 'reunion' did not materialise. I subsequently found out she had gone back to her husband in a last-ditch attempt to make things work. As devastated as I was, I fully understood her need to do the right thing by her kids; the paradox being, although I totally embraced this value, it felt so wrong.

The next day, I was sitting on my settee – feeling like a besotted, love-sick puppy – when the doorbell rang and yes, you're right, it was Lorraine. She bounced into my arms and blurted out that she'd tried to make things work, but just couldn't do it anymore. Despite this emotional euphoria, there was still a big part of my life missing – my kids.

Shortly afterwards, I moved in with Lorraine. We started to gel as a family and even managed to get some voluntary work. Slowly but surely, I started to get my confidence and self-respect back.

My identity as a strong, but sensitive and caring family man was beginning to emerge again.

One thing I know for sure, is that prosperity is usually associated with people's financial wealth but for me, this couldn't be further from the truth. The love and security we shared as a family – spanning nearly two decades – was absolutely priceless.

Although the voluntary work we were doing at the Greenway Centre in Sneinton, Nottingham wasn't rewarding money-wise, it was definitely providing power to know that we were serving the community and people that were less fortunate than ourselves.

In 1999, Lorraine and I were blessed with a beautiful daughter of our own – Julia, and life seemed very idyllic.

Add-in the progression of then having the confidence to start my own business – repairing & selling computers – and prosperity did pleasantly start to present financial rewards; we felt abundant!

This was eventually supplemented by Lorraine getting a job with the local council and progressing along nicely.

However – after nearly two decades – I became aware that things between us were changing; I began to consistently feel we had no common purpose anymore and I found myself asking a lot of questions once again, about my identity and 'Who Am I?'

This time though, it was different; I intuitively became aware that I was capable of being so much more in my life – for the first time in ages, this was no longer about Lorraine or the family. It was about me and the realisation that a new phase of my life was unfolding – like a butterfly emerging from the caterpillar.

Early in 2017, Lorraine assertively confirmed what I already knew – it was over between us and the pain of delivering this crushing news was alleviated somewhat by me agreeing we had drifted apart and become totally different people.

For weeks after, I found myself in a crazy world of uncertainty and emotional chaos. All the certainty I had ever known, had now vanished; I was running on 'emotional fumes' and there were times when I didn't know if I had the strength to survive the moment – let alone the day!

I kept sliding into victim mode and if it wasn't for the continuous interventions of my loving family & friends – including Paul Lowe – I can categorically assert that I would not be here to recall the journey of my life.

After working through my recent pain and suffering, I'm now embracing my emerging identity as a warrior; one that will use my many rich life experiences to continue to grow and more importantly, pass on the lessons learnt, for the benefit of others.

WOW: It's better to be a loving warrior than a lonely worrier

searceykevin62@gmail.com

Colleen Williamson (Canada)

The Power Of Pain

Life offers many challenges and pain can be an insurmountable part of the journey. The choices you make in any given moment will determine your path for the future. The choice is yours, and until you understand that you really do have the power within you to create a better life, you may suffer as a victim unnecessarily.

Having lived through the many challenges that life has to offer, do you ever find yourself asking 'Why is this happening to me?' 'Why can't my life just be different?' 'Why do I have to live through so much pain?'

Over the last couple of years, I have become keenly aware of patterns that ran consistently throughout my life, resulting from the choices that I made years ago. Most recently, I discovered the impact of an early experience in my childhood and how I negatively interpreted that meaning into my own self-worth.

Growing up – the youngest of 4 children – I was a shy and very emotional little girl; being an 'Army Brat our family relocated often, finally to settle down in the city at the tender age of 5. We moved into a little yellow house in a quiet crescent, a neighbourhood which I called home for the next 10 years.

My secure childhood as I knew it, was about to change. My earliest memory of emotional pain, was about to be the beginning of my life's challenges because of how I perceived the experience in my own mind.

I remember sitting on my bed – in an upstairs bedroom that I shared with my sister – and although I don't remember the exact words, the memory remains clear in my mind; my Mom sat beside me as she gently explained what was about to change my life forever. Unknowingly the divorce of my parents would affect how I would make decisions for the rest of my life.

When you experience a traumatic situation, you make 'Key Decisions' that help you rationalize what has just happened and why. Those key decisions become your sub-conscious survival mechanisms. The feelings of unworthiness, rejection and guilt that I somehow caused my Dad to leave our family were the meanings that I attached to that moment in my life.

This was a heavy burden for a young child to have to carry for so many years; although I recall some happy memories growing up with both of my parents. Camping with my Dad and his new family during the summer was a highlight; there was always something fun to do.

I also remember crying when it was time to say goodbye, the pain resurfacing each time. My parents were good, hardworking people, dealing with their own lives; they did the best they could.

My Mom often tired after a long day at work, would rest before supper. She seemed exhausted taking care of 4 kids while working full-time. Looking back I realize that I may have tried to be the mother figure; being the emotional caring type of person that I was, I must have sensed her struggle.

As we grew older, all four of us kids took our turns making dinner and doing household chores. I remember learning how to grocery shop at a young age on my own. I would walk six blocks to shop for the groceries that were on the list for that week, fill out and pay by a cheque that my mom had provided, then take a taxi home.

Mom did a good job of teaching us how to be responsible, how to cook and the value of a dollar. Interesting how two of us became chefs and one a baker. I was popular, active and participated in sports throughout my school years. It gave me the feeling of connection to people, that I strived to have.

Growing up, I spent a lot of time with my best friend; we lived close to each other and are good friends still to this day. Junior High school started shifting things in my life; my friend and I would sneak out at night and we got into our share of trouble. We never did anything illegal; we were your typical rebellious teenagers.

My first heartbreak came in Junior High; I fell head over heels for a boy during the summer holidays – only to be rejected by him after I became pregnant. He was a year older and going onto high school. No matter how hard I tried to get his attention he wanted nothing more to do with me.

The pain of that rejection took me years to get over; I was devastated, ashamed and felt unworthy and left wondering what I had done wrong. Ridden with guilt and the shame of becoming pregnant at such a young age, I made the most difficult decision of my life, to give away my baby boy.

I felt unworthy of taking care of him; somehow I felt responsible enough to know that the right decision was to give him the chance at a better life than I was capable of providing.

I had to believe in my heart that a life with two responsible, more stable parents was the best chance for him, as devastating and painful as it was.

This – I have come to realize – is where I had created the feelings of not wanting to be seen; not allowing myself to be heard and burying my feelings deep inside of me, as it was such a lonely, uncertain and devastating time in my life.

I always wondered what other people were saying about me; everyone in my life carried on as if nothing had happened. The fact that I gave away a child was never discussed. I was ashamed and I held onto this pain for many years, never dealing with the loss of a part of me – a child that I have not had the courage to try to find, still to this day.

Feeling the need to be in the company of my friends, I began to stay out past curfew. I wasn't trying to be a difficult teenager, I was just struggling to ease the pain of what had just happened in my life; trying desperately to fit in again and regain some sort of a normal life.

At times it was just awkward; it was as if nothing had happened, although everyone knew. This part of my life was never talked about again. It was as if a part of me died and I was unable to grieve, or at least I didn't know how.

After a few months my parents decided that it was best that I go live with my Dad in a small town two hours away. I was now at a point in my life whereby I really didn't want to move and leave my friends. It became too difficult for my Mom as I was depressed and started missing school.

I couldn't grasp anything; learning was a challenge and I had become too much of a burden at home. Starting High School in a small town was different; everyone knew everybody else's business. I made a few friends and life continued, although it wasn't long and I met someone two years older than me.

I began to stay out late and disobey the rules once again. Within a year I ran away from home and moved several hours away with my new boyfriend. I dropped out of high school and it seemed as though following through with anything that would move me forward in life wasn't important enough.

Therefore I wasn't worthy of making something of myself, it was always a struggle, continually self-sabotaging any efforts for success throughout my life.

The relationship quickly became controlling; I felt alone and trapped in an abusive situation far away from anyone that I knew.

I felt I was manipulated to stay with lies that he was dying. It was a struggle for nine years; fear became constant and I was convinced that I wouldn't amount to anything, so why should I even try. I felt stuck and was frozen with fear.

I was completely exhausted; I analysed everything to avoid starting an argument. Instead of wanting to be with people, now I began to isolate myself from everyone. Alcohol and drugs were consistent and brought out the anger in him and the fear in me.

The feelings of shame crept in even more; I thought I must have done something to deserve this. 'I don't know what to do' became a statement I repeated often while in distress, without realizing the impact it would have on my life. That statement affected who I was, and how I made decisions moving forward.

Looking back, I see the effects it placed on my sub-conscious mind. I lacked confidence, clarity and have always had a difficult time making decisions; often procrastinating. Because I burned into my mind 'I don't know what to do' it kept me stuck for years.

I was numb to the pain of constant verbal, emotional and physical abuse. Being lied to and cheated on, I wondered, 'Was I really that bad a person?' 'Why was this happening to me?' I distanced myself from my family as I felt ashamed that I had let them down.

After several attempts to leave, I would invariably return back to the same familiar patterns of abuse. It took nine years until I finally became strong enough to break free. As difficult as it was, my confidence was beaten down and any self-esteem was non-existent.

I felt much older than my years and I was only 25. I intuitively knew I had to protect my two children from being affected any further, they had already seen too much. I was beginning to realize that my life was not normal, and being a victim of domestic violence had to stop.

I have found myself in more dysfunctional long-term relationships since then; becoming involved with someone new immediately after ending the previous one. This never allowed the chance to heal any part of my life as a person or to be a better Mom for my children.

The relationships never felt truly fulfilling. It was as if I was trying to fill a void in my life. I couldn't commit to marriage, much like many things in my life; committing to something for me personally was difficult. Although when I gave my word to someone else, or to an employer, I would give everything of myself, to the point of being a perfectionist and workaholic.

When I was 35 years old, my Dad was diagnosed with cancer. I watched as he suffered; it was extremely hard for me to see him in such pain because he had always been a strong and disciplined man. The cancer took his life and he died of Multiple Myeloma. I became extremely depressed with no energy to function.

Losing my Dad created immense sorrow in me that lasted for years. I remember thinking the thoughts 'Why did he leave so soon?' 'Did I cause him to die?' 'It should have been me' as I felt I was the unworthy one.

The grief of his death consumed me to the point that two years later, I was diagnosed with Stage 3 Non-Hodgkins Lymphoma, which soon turned into Stage 4. The treatment wasn't working and now I had my own battle and for two years fought for my life.

I feared what would happen to my children; they needed me and I wasn't ready to die.

Pain is inevitable – long-term suffering is not; emotional pain can control you if you allow it. When you focus on what you don't want, you bring more of exactly that into your life. Focusing on what's going wrong can become an addiction, where you seek out the people and events that will keep you in that familiar state.

Even though you know you don't want that kind of life, you are almost certain you can rely on what's going to happen, so you stay stuck in the cycle. Often people will stay in an unhealthy situation, rather than risk feeling uncomfortable moving into the unknown, even if the latter is a better option.

Overcoming the challenges and struggles in my life, I have become very aware of why things happened and what meanings I attached to the events of my past. I have come to realize the answer always lies within me; not from any external source or validation.

Surviving cancer was a turning point in my life; something inside of me woke up and I started a new journey of personal growth – one that still continues to this day.

Over the years, I have immersed myself in personal development and spiritual growth, incorporating meditation, neuroplasticity and several healing modalities into my life.

I have become certified in the Tony Robbins Coaching Program and more recently a Trainer and Certified Coach in Brainsweep Systems, a powerful brain technique that has the ability to limit and relieve the effects of trauma in all areas of your life.

I have come to know that pain is an inevitable part of your life; however learning how to heal your emotional pain is something we must all do.

> WOW: If sharing your own vulnerabilities can inspire one person, that can be the most powerful healing of all, and I believe…the best legacy you can leave!

Gurveer Khabra (UK)

Dare To Dream – Dare To Hope

First of all, I'd like to thank Paul D. Lowe for inviting me to share my chapter in the Speaking From Our Hearts book series. I'm so grateful to participate, especially with so many amazing co-authors.

Rejection

When I was twenty years old, I was with my friends at a night-club. They were dancing with girls, and some eventually left with them. But I couldn't because I had less self-confidence. I have consistently been rejected with harsh words. Not just once, but time after time – including that dreadful experience at the night-club. The knock-on from this, was I quit going out and socialising; I felt very uncomfortable with myself and decided to go to the library to write my stories instead. I had sworn that I will always be in a friend zone with a girl, not more than that. I started to feel really unattractive and like I didn't deserve to be in a relationship… or so I thought.

Until I met 'the girl' in the library. I won't reveal her real name, for the sake of her privacy.

Two years later, I was in the library off Belgrave Road in my home-town of Leicester, in the UK. I was reading the Hindu Scripture holy book called the *Mahabharata*, with stories of heroes, villains, virtues, and gods. I learned so much knowledge from that book. I loved the story of the character named Karna, who was son of the god Surya and the princess Kunti. I could strongly relate to his character, especially being a loyal friend and keeping promises. My loved ones referred me to the golden heart in the book.

As I read, I noticed a girl walking towards me, so I quickly looked at my book. She then placed herself opposite me. I was feeling nervous, then heard her calling for someone, which may have been her friend, or her boyfriend. Then she called out again – it was so unique.

I looked up to see this girl, a beautiful Indian girl, with black long straight hair and dark brownish skin. Her smile radiated her inner beauty.

She then introduced herself as Aarti. She wanted to know about the book I was reading; I calmly told her about it. As time flew by, I started feeling comfortable with her. I never felt this before in front of a girl. At 7pm, we exited the library together, and I kept on telling her about the book. We then arrived at her home – close to the library – where she waved bye to me, as I did the same. At the time I felt shy.

Later, at the temple of Ram Mandir on McDonald Road – while attending the annual Hindu festival of Navaratri, which happens every autumn – I saw Aarti again, and went to greet her. She saw me and smiled. Immediately, I felt courage and confidence with her. I dared to dream. My facial expression changed into attraction towards her, like the character of Joey from the TV show "Friends," who smiles in a certain way, as he says his well-known line…

"Hey, how you doin'?"

Aarti blushed at seeing me.

I did something I rarely did with girls in those days… I looked at her while, before daring to mutter a few words. Ever since a pretty and popular girl warned me when I was at college not to look at her because I had scary eyes, I didn't look at girls – but I looked at Aarti.

Suddenly someone whacked me on the back! I spun around to see who it was, and Aarti did, too. We both thought it was her brother, but it was my sister holding a small bar in her hands.

I wanted to ask her why she hit me, but instead, I introduced them to each other. Aarti greeted my sister, before she then asked me to dance with her. Surprised, I asked my sister to join us, but she refused, preferring to be with her new friends. So, I agreed to join Aarti doing a Hindu ancestral dance called Garba. The dance is to pay respect to the goddesses by dancing from clapping and swinging around the floor.

After the event, my sister and I were outside waiting for our cab and said goodbye to our friends. Sometime later, Aarti came out of the temple with her brother. She then introduced us to him, but from looking at his scowl, I knew he wasn't happy with me.

Then our cab arrived; we waved goodbye and went home. As we arrived home, I asked my sister why she whacked me. She assertively replied…

"You looked at that her like players do, that's why, and you did that in front of her brother."

I was shocked. I couldn't believe it! I wondered how I could even look at Aarti, who was beautiful like those popular girls in college.

Not A Player

After that, I bumped into Aarti on many occasions. For example, once at the clock tower in the town, we walked past each other, each accompanied by our friends. Another time, when I was on Belgrave Road walking home with my friends, I spotted Aarti, and I stopped to say hello to her. My friends kept walking on their way, but Aarti and I gazed at each other for a while. Somehow I just knew deep inside that she liked it – and so did I.

On another beautiful afternoon, I was in my room writing my story when my sister called and invited me to join her, and also her friend, at her friend's shop at City Centre. I refused because I was in the middle of writing.

Her friend got on the line. It was Aarti! She requested that I come. I couldn't refuse!

In record time I excitedly arrived at the 'shop destination'. Aarti and my sister smiled, clearly pleased to see me. I hoped I looked at Aarti in a friendly way and not as a 'player'.

Aarti looked at me and blushed while talking to my sister. The latter took me aside and said we should leave because Aarti was still working. Plus, the manager might give her a lecture for standing around chatting us up. We left before we had a chance to say goodbye to her.

I should mention that at this time, gang members were targeting me. A few days later my sister passed on a threatening message from the gang:

"If we see you on Belgrave Road, you'll be sorry."

Full of fear, I still went to the library to return a book.

Hiding out in the library, I was reading a book when someone called me from behind. It was Aarti. I tried to ignore her and thought she might be involved.

She called my name, again and again.

I then whirled around and pretended I was my own twin brother with a fake name, Gurvlee. Aarti didn't believe me. However, she pretended to play along with me. I then started to complain about my 'brother' Gurveer.

I asked Aarti to pass on the message to my 'brother', and she agreed, though she must have been very confused – I know I was! Feeling bad for involving her in my trickery, I went home.

The next morning, my sister and I were just leaving the Shires, the local mall, when who should we run into but Aarti. She greeted my sister with a smile on her face but ignored me.

My sister looked completely confused, before quizzically asking…

"Why are you ignoring Gurveer?"

Aarti then turned to give me a smirk, before turning her back on me and informing my sister that I had lied to her about the twin brothers. My sister tried explaining the situation with the gang, including my belief that Aarti was involved, while I apologised for lying.

Aarti – still upset with me, despite the explanation – seemed to understand my sister and said…

"I know why he lied to others, but he shouldn't lie to me."

She then mentioned that she was no longer a friend of the girl who sent the gang after me. That relieved my mind.

As we exited the Shires, Aarti giggled at me, with a smile, and said: "You're a liar."

She invited us to go bowling with her. We both asked if we could invite close friends, and Aarti accepted our request. She then told us to meet her in the afternoon. We agreed. in the afternoon, we arrived at the bowling club, where Aarti and her five friends greeted us. She then took me to bowl a few games with her friend;

I felt like a special person for the first time.

I felt like a million dollars when I knocked all those pins down, but I didn't realise then, that Aarti was my lucky charm, also giving me a positive attitude. I felt like one of those popular guys at my college who have a bunch of girls around them.

Imagine my surprise when my sister told me to ask Aarti out for a date. I looked so shocked and denied that Aarti was more than a friend.

My sister mentioned that every moment Aarti always had her eyes on me. I didn't believe
that Aarti would like me that way, and only saw me as a friend. But my sister wouldn't give up, so I 'surrendered' to the idea.

I walked towards Aarti and asked to speak in private. We walked off and found a spot away from the others. I felt so nervous and uncomfortable with her. I was going to ask her out for the first time and also break the friend code. Something told me inside that if I did this, there would be no mending our friendship and she might not like me anymore or want me around her. Worst of all, she might send her brother after me. I felt goosebumps, but when she smiled, I asked her out, bluntly.

Her response was equally blunt…

"I was waiting for you to ask me out, what took you so long?" she said.

As I heard her reply and couldn't believe it, my smile nearly appeared, but then she continued by mentioning that she has a boyfriend.

My heart sinking, I congratulated her with a smile and apologised for asking her out. I could picture her being happy with him, instead of me. I then imagined him: better looking than me, and earns a lot, with a sports car, and lots of other crazy imaginings.

I walked to my sister and friends – they saw my face and knew it was bad news. I asked them if we could leave.

They said farewell and I couldn't even face Aarti; being full of embarrassment for breaking the friendship code.

When I arrived home, I promised myself I would never see Aarti ever again.

My sister asked if I was okay and I pretended that I wasn't bothered at all, but deep down I was. I lost a good friend by asking her out. I couldn't be her friend anymore because of an oath I made to myself in secondary school. After being heartbroken, I pledged, "I will never take a girl away from her boyfriend."

I moved on by avoiding the library I loved because there was always a chance that I might see Aarti there. Looking back, I realize I gave up.

Four years later, according to my parents' wishes, I was married in an arranged marriage.

Life Without Love

One day, when I was 25 and with my one-year-old son in town, I bumped into Aarti! I was so shocked to see her, and she did not seem happy to see me. I shared all that had happened to me while we were apart.

I then asked about the relationship with her boyfriend and also about her life in general.

Aarti told me she was a supervisor, at the rugby store for Leicester Tigers. She mentioned a lot about her life, with one exception. She said nothing about her boyfriend.

We then reached her store on Market Street.

I asked for her number so we could catch up…

"No, you lost the chance to ask me that now," she said.

I was confused about what she meant about that.

She said nothing more on that topic and went inside the store while I stood looking totally confused. I turned around to walk off, but then felt someone was watching me, so I turned around and see Aarti framed by the glass door, tears rolling down on her cheeks.

She quickly wiped her face and walked to the back room. I was so concerned about her and wanted to know why she was crying. I wanted to knock on the door to ask her why she was upset, but I decided to go home. I was still thinking about my friend.

After months had gone by, with me still living without love, I went to see her at the store. She was behind the counter and upset. I walked up and started asking about her relationship with her boyfriend.

She responded that they were fine and asked about the relationship with my wife; I falsely replied that she was treating me so well. However, I sensed she might know I was lying to her (again).

We started having a conversation about so many subjects. I could see something was bothering her. In the course of the conversation, she asked me about my job at a bed and breakfast off Narborough Road. I told her that they fired me for no reason, and it was not my fault.

In a friendly way, she advised me that I would find a better job. Gratefully, I thanked her, said farewell, and left the store. I hadn't gone more than a few steps away from the store when my gut feeling warned me that she would be leaving me soon.

I then stupidly took a picture of her on my phone. She caught me and called me back inside the store. I couldn't explain why I did that. My reasons were so complicated and messy. Upset, she demanded to know why I did that, and I denied doing it.

She ordered me to go because she knew I was lying to her. I walked out and felt like a horrible man and not a good friend. I asked myself over and over why I did that.

That night, my mind wouldn't leave me in peace; I felt in turmoil as punishment for my lie to Aarti.

The next day I went to clear the air with her and ask for forgiveness. Aarti wasn't happy with me and scolded me…

"Never lie to someone who has feelings for you."

After she calmed herself down, she put a smile back on her face and asked about my job search. I told her my wife wouldn't help me at all, but I showed her an application form for a job as a male cleaner at well-known leisure centre and asked her if she would help me.

She said yes!

After we completed the form, I felt deep gratitude for her help. I was just about to leave the store when Aarti advised me, smiling,

"Always stand up for your rights." I agreed to her advice and said farewell to her with a smile on my face. I was so happy that we are friends again – I dared to hope.

After my interview, I got selected. The first friend I wanted to tell was Aarti. I rushed to her store, and when I arrived, she wasn't there. I asked her manager where she was. He ignored me and walked away to serve another customer. Confused, I wanted answers about Aarti not being present.

I pulled aside a blonde assistant, and pleaded, "Where is Aarti?"

The assistant replied very harshly, that Aarti had left the city.

I felt my heart was going to slip away and I felt my tears were going to come, so I walked out of the shop. On the way home, I searched for her. In my mind I carried an image of her adorable smile and her fingers waving, and the memory of every moment we spent together as friends.

Too late, I realised that my feelings for her weren't just friendship. They were more than that. Now I felt deep regret.

A few months later, I heard from a mutual friend that Aarti had already broken up with her boyfriend in the last year. My world shattered upon hearing that and in my pain, I wished I didn't get married to an ungrateful wife. If only I married Aarti, who would be a better wife. I lost my opportunity with a very special person.

It's been 13 years and I'm finally divorced from the heartless ex-wife. I sometimes imagine that I am married to Aarti. I think about her and wish I could share all my stories with her and share all the things that are precious to her.

I would like to add a brief message to all women out there: some guys don't approach a girl, because they fear rejection. They fear someone will hurt their feelings. Let that guy know that you are interested. And to any guy out there who cares about someone special, I say, "Dare to dream and dare to hope."

I dare to dream about and hope for love!

Cherri Forsyth (South Africa)

From Hell To Healing

Our lives were irrevocably changed on February 17th 2002 when our youngest daughter Kerry died, aged 9. She died following an operation to remove a non-malignant tumour from her pituitary gland. When the doctor told us she was brain dead, I just remember grabbing his hand, with a long moan of NOOOOO!

We left the hospital numbly that morning, with achingly empty arms, and returned to a home without our Kerry; our 'bubble of joy and enthusiasm'. Previously our home had been alive with the sounds of her excited chatter, and now we were plunged into a hollow silence.

I woke up every day for many months afterwards feeling that I had experienced a terrible nightmare –consistently thinking 'oh how awful, I know it will go away when I wake up', only to find it crushingly true, day after day. It felt like part of me had been viciously ripped away.

I now had to adjust to our new 'normal', with my husband Mike and older daughter Cathleen. Words don't even come close to describing how I felt – shattered into a million little bits, bleak, heavy, overwhelmed, with waves of excruciating pain at the thought of living the rest of my live without her; physical pain in my heart, and how I cried and cried.

I didn't know there could be so many tears in one person. I often spent the day in raw tears; the pain, longing, pining, missing, were all just too much. I felt my sobs coming from deep within my gut; fuelling deep moans of anguish. I just couldn't stop it...it came, and came, and came!

Initially there was a lot of care from our community, but gradually – as is to be expected – it dried up. By this time, my husband Mike was also unable to speak about the loss of Kerry. I found myself isolated and surrounded in a dark swirl of pain, loneliness, and felt shunned by others.

It was like I had become someone else because of the loss of our daughter; people who used to greet me, now suddenly pretended they didn't know me. Adding to the pain of our loss, we sadly lost relationships with dear friends and family – pain on top of pain!

I can only think that they thought losing a child was contagious, or that they wanted us to be the same people we were before Kerry died – which was obviously impossible; how could anyone be the same after so much suffering, dealing with such fracturing grief?

About three months after the death of Kerry, I noticed a change in Mike. He was suddenly very angry and volatile. It started off with an incident once a month, became once a week, to eventually many times a week. My quiet and peace-loving husband had become a 'monster man'.

The only person who could really understand the loss of Kerry was my fellow parent, my fellow sufferer, my husband and yet he cut himself off completely, and in his place was this man who regularly shouted at me, blamed me for everything, was frighteningly irrational in arguments, who had to always be right and accused me of all sorts of things.

He was a complete stranger – where was the old Mike I loved? Where was my fellow empathiser – my beloved husband? He paid lip-service to psychologists and lied to them, so they thought he was dealing well with the death; meanwhile he had become very abusive towards me.

Imagine my incredulity – a kind, loving man had transformed into an angry, abusive, yelling, volatile, cold man. He reserved his appalling behaviour only for me – outwardly he was as charming as ever! Now in addition to my own grief, I was dealing with a stranger in our marriage.

As I fought to save our marriage, I was confronted with more and more bizarre behaviour from Mike, which made me wonder if I was losing my mind. I particularly recall – after one all-night fight between us – he whistled off to work the next day, leaving me in a miserable huddle on our veranda; sobbing as I watched him go off to work.

When he came home that night, and I mentioned that we needed to resolve the issue from our fight, he asked, "Which fight?", and when I replied, "The all-night one", he said that it hadn't happened! His behaviour was so awful that he couldn't admit to it to himself, so he just denied that it had ever happened.

If he admitted to it, he would have to do something about it, and he didn't have the capacity to engage with his shadow side, with Monster Man!

My husband was totally fractured, and I feared for his mental health. Another worry was added to my already over-burdened shoulders.

He seemed to have no worries at all in the world, but his eyes betrayed him – they were dead at their core. As our marriage deteriorated more and more, he became even more volatile. He then took to ignoring me. It was as if I didn't exist; wasn't living in the same house as him.

I was expecting him to take me to hospital for a minor day surgery – he forgot, so I drove myself. When he came home and I had a plaster over my nose, he pretended like he didn't see it, didn't ask me how I was, let alone apologise for forgetting!

Being ignored was telling me that I was worthless, not important enough for his attention, a nothing. Being ignored is one of the cruellest things you can do to another. From feeling a treasured, loved and worthy wife, I had been demoted to a nothing, an invisible being.

I still battled on – fighting for a marriage I didn't even know if I wanted anymore, and every step of the way was being thwarted by Mike. This battle continued for eight years, with our marriage heading further and further into dysfunction, definitely heading for the death of what was once a marriage that many aspired to.

I was exhausted to my core, and bewildered. I had put my own grief journey on hold in order to put my emotional energy into caring for Mike, and then trying to save our marriage, and yet all I received was abuse, blame, and accusations.

I fought so hard because I knew this Monster Man was the result of Mike not dealing appropriately with the loss of Kerry, and that once he allowed himself to grieve, then he would start healing, and then hopefully our marriage could recover.

During all of these eight years, I never gave up hope – I always knew it would come right.

However in 2010 – the year we both turned 50 and Cathleen turned 21, he had an affair. The pain of this betrayal was the very last straw to me. I finally lost all hope. A year which should have been filled with celebration was filled with barren-ness, pain, anger, rejection and disbelief.

Our teetering marriage now absolutely shattered – there was nothing left anymore. I really, really didn't care about him, our marriage, myself. I was in an emotional vacuum – realising it was my brain protecting me from the pain of the awful situation which had manifested.

I had fought so hard to save the marriage I had treasured. I now crumbled, collapsed and my heart shattered into bits I felt I could never put together again. I wasn't sure I could ever recover from this. I had valued my relationship and marriage above all other things, and now this too had collapsed – shattered.

I had lost our daughter, some friends, some family members and now our marriage too. What was left of me now? How much pain was I to endure? It was as if I had been flattened time and time again; like being run over by a ten-ton truck, and just as I was standing up again, the next truck would arrive and flatten me again, and again and again…

Eventually it was taking me longer and longer to start gathering my resources and stand up between the 'after-shocks'. Maybe it would just be easier to remain lying on the ground, then I wouldn't have to invest all my energy in getting up between the knocks…if I just lay there, I wouldn't have very far to fall each time!

I requested that Mike leave our family home when I found out about his affair. My life was grey, without hope, without laughter. Just an endless nothingness – nothing to excite me, nothing to look forward to, nothing to live for, nothing …nothing…nothing…

Looking back it was very scary for me to feel nothing – I am sensitive and always care and feel so much. Suddenly the Sahara Desert had nothing on me! I was in a barren, heavy, dark, imbalanced and very unhappy place.

Gradually I could see the darkness begin to lift, and let the light in.

My rays of sunshine were our daughter Cath, my parents and sister, my sister-in-law, a few friends and my work as a Life Coach. Other than that, life was totally meaningless to me; so now came a time of profound introspection. What had this journey taught me? What was life all about? What was important to me?

Could I teach myself to care again? Could I teach myself to be passionate about anything ever again? Could I ever laugh again? Where was I headed to now?

I started to put myself back together again – slowly. I took a few months off work, and took time to be very gentle with myself; spent many hours reading and growing in knowledge, doing anything to soothe my jangling soul – finding my mojo.

I slowly began exercising again, spending time with my family and trusted friends, but mainly pondering and thinking and pondering some more; always listening to very beautiful music.

I woke up one day with a flutter of excitement in my heart, (very short-lived) and I knew then that I was healing, and that I would be ok. I had found out what my priorities were; I had found out who I was, what my values were, what I was prepared to put up with (or not) and what kind of life I wanted to live – with or without Mike.

I realised I had overcome one of my greatest fears – the fear of being on my own. I could be happy on my own – I was a strong, independent woman. The strong steel core inside me had bent, but didn't break!

So what happened to Mike, and our marriage? Well, Mike got really ill (and remains so until today) with a serious, chronic and rare autoimmune disease, as well as diabetes.

This was caused by stress – the stress of living a lie, of trying to pretend that everything was fine; that he was coping well with the loss of Kerry. He finally underwent a powerful awakening, became conscious and experienced a metamorphosis.

It was almost as if he had been living in a mist of fantasy, a mist of make-believe, and now as the veil fell from his eyes he could see who he had become, the damage he had caused, the trust he had shattered, the hurt he had caused – all the things of value that he had thrown away.

He started on a major programme of personal development, and slowly and painfully, a different man began to emerge.

He became conscious, achingly aware of how he had been living since Kerry died. He allowed all the thoughts he had been blocking, to flood his soul, and a profound change became apparent.

He painfully transformed himself into a conscious and aware being, and in doing so became aware of all the things Monster Man had destroyed. He could no longer deny all of the awful things. Courageously he had to look at the very worst of himself, didn't like what he saw, and worked very hard to change them.

I saw Mike putting effort into himself and our marriage, and gradually my very injured and bruised heart warmed a little to him. I had never stopped loving him. However, I was still guarding my heart – it had been stomped on too many times, but I started entertaining the thought of being together with him again.

After a six-month separation, we got back together. We have both worked very hard to re-build our marriage. We have used the hardship to weather ourselves and our marriage into something even more beautiful than it was before.

We have both become strong individually, and hence together we are even stronger than before. We meditate together every morning, both work from home, take time each day to enjoy life and each other, socialise, and live a life filled with hard-won peace and love.

We now have a marriage characterised by love, laughter, authenticity, honesty, kindness, joy and connection. We will be celebrating 33 years of marriage in September 2021.

WOW: The power of perseverance –
never give up on something you truly believe in

https://cherriforsythcoaching.com

Jennifer Hyde (UK)

A Personal View Of Hope

A chance conversation led me to share that embarking on a third marriage personified for me the phrase '**the triumph of hope over experience**'.

This dialogue led me to think about hope from both my personal point of view, and seen through the quotes of famous and not-so-famous people.

All human wisdom is summed up in two words: wait and hope (Alexander Dumas)

Hope is a word that we often use without thinking and when what is hoped for does not materialise, there is no great consequence, for example:

"I hope it won't rain today."

"I hope my parcel will arrive soon."

Yet, hope is also a word that can carry a much deeper meaning, depending on our current circumstances, especially true in relation to life-threatening illness:

"I hope the operation will be successful."

"I hope this time the treatment will work."

Hope is important because it can make the present moment less difficult to bear.

If we believe that tomorrow will be better, we can bear a hardship today. (Thich Nhat Hanh)

Think about the difference in emphasis, during the Covid pandemic, when you hear or see the words:

"I hope we can get our holiday this year."

"I hope I will still have a job and be able to pay my bills at the end of all this."

"I hope my seriously ill loved-one will survive this terrible disease."

Hope for a return to 'normality' is what has kept many people, including myself, going during these exceptional times, while others have struggled to cope. That is not to say the latter have given up hope, just that they are finding today's hardships more difficult to deal with.

Whatever the disappointments Covid has brought, especially in relation to not being able to spend time with my family, my own mantra has been, *"I do not have Covid, and nor does anyone in my family, so we are lucky"* and obviously my own hope is that this situation will continue.

I am prepared for the worst, but hope for the best.
(Benjamin Disraeli)

Many years ago a greatly-loved, elderly family member had a major and devastating stroke. For many months I hoped this wonderful person would make some type of recovery; constantly hoping for the best while I was unprepared for the worst. However as time went on, watching her pain and distress, my hope of what would be the best, changed. I stopped hoping for the outcome that would be the best for me, to have her back as she was before; instead, I began to accept this was never going to happen and I prepared myself for what would be the worst for me. I started to hope for an end to her suffering, something that was the best for her. This shift in the object of my hope was very difficult to live with for a long time.

When the world says, "give up," hope whispers, "try it one more time." (Not attributed)

Aside from situations where hope enables people to desire a better future, it can also play a major part when individuals are looking for their current situation to improve:

"I hope today I will not do or say something that will make him/ her angry..."

"I hope today will be the day that he/ she doesn't steal from me when they visit..."

In these circumstances how often do we hear from family or friends "Why do you put up with it? Why do you keep letting them do this to you? How many times have we heard it said, mistakenly attributed to Einstein, that the definition of insanity is doing the same thing over and over again and expecting a different result?

Yet, in the realm of personal and professional relationships, this is not as straightforward as it might sound.

Hope, in its most powerful sense, often plays a part in an individual's reluctance to walk away from a damaging relationship or work situation. Despite previous experience(s), we continue to hope that next time will be different. Without the hope that an abusive person may change, or a beloved family member may stop stealing from your purse, what is left, except perhaps, fear of the future?

May your choices reflect your hopes, not your fears.
(Nelson Mandela)

To recognise that it has been in vain to hope for things to change, whether in a relationship or a work situation, means choices have to be made – in the words of the song, *"Do I stay or do I go?"*

Like many people I worked hard to pursue a career path and achieve a senior role I absolutely loved. Unfortunately after some years, my dream role was blighted by a new line-manager whose approach was to undermine and criticise anyone who did not completely agree with everything he said or did. His command-and-control style of management was in complete contrast to my own approach to leadership where I focussed on empowering staff, showing them respect for sharing their views and ideas, even when I disagreed with them.

Eventually, after many months, I came to the realisation that no matter how hard I worked and how much I hoped his behaviour would change, it was never going to. So I made the difficult choice to walk away, fearful of not having a job to go to, whilst also feeling that my confidence had been damaged to such an extent that I would never be able to claw my way back from the very low place I had reached. It took quite some time before new hopes for the future outweighed those fears.

**Most of the important things in the world have been
accomplished by people who have kept on trying
when there seemed to be no hope at all.
(Dale Carnegie)**

One response to the devastating economic impact of the Covid pandemic has been the recommendation that people should stop seeking work in sectors they have been used to, particularly those where the impact of Covid has been most damaging, and start looking elsewhere.

So hope has become an important factor in the lives of many unemployed people. The hope that the next job application will be successful, even though they may have no experience in that sector and are competing against the many others who do have experience but have lost their jobs over the past year. To maintain hope after the fifth, tenth, or twentieth unsuccessful application or interview requires a certain resilience which becomes harder to maintain as time goes on. Yet again, without genuine hope, what is left?

**It's always something to know you've done the most
you could. But don't leave off hoping, or it's of no use
doing anything. Hope, hope to the last!
(Charles Dickens)**

At one point in my life, I received 17 rejections before being successful in getting a job interview. Although I hoped each time my application would be successful, I also researched as much information as I could on how to write effective applications and/ or amended my CV as seemed necessary. Every time I believed I had done the most I could, and I kept on hoping for a better outcome. However, hope alone is sometimes not enough; in some circumstances it has to be supported by actions designed to increase the chances of success.

Repeated failure can require much soul-searching; *what could I have done differently? Where did I go wrong?* And sometimes comes the realisation that actually you haven't done anything wrong, it's just that someone else did it differently and their way suited what the recruiters were looking for. Therefore, there is the hope that next time you will be the person the recruiters are seeking.

We should not let our fears hold us back from pursuing our hopes. (John F Kennedy)

Returning to my own triumph of hope over experience by marrying for a third time, I can share that it did however, take me almost 20 years to overcome my fears and grow comfortable enough with myself to take the risk that this time all would be well.

Three grand essentials to happiness in this life are something to do, something to love, and something to hope for. (Joseph Addison)

I wholeheartedly agree with Addison's view. My *something to do* is to always be learning. My *something to love* is my husband and wonderful family. Lastly, my *something to hope for* is success in my new profession as an Executive and Career Coach.

What do you hope for?

http://www.mjh-coaching.com

Martin Leifeld (USA)

Hope

The definition of hope that I prefer for its simplicity – to expect with confidence – I found in The Merriam-Webster Dictionary. This uncomplicated description of hope defines the hope that has accompanied me throughout my life, giving impetus to personal and professional growth and development. It has been a powerful and positive undercurrent flowing within me. Hope goes before me, inspiring me to press on into the future, into the unknown, day-by-day, year-by-year.

Hopeful Parents

I believe I was born hopeful. I credit my parents with instilling hope within my five siblings and me. As far back as I can recall I have generally enjoyed a positive outlook. That is not to deny that there have been plenty of times, amid trials and challenges, that I have struggled to preserve a sense of hope.

My parents Matt and Marian Leifeld were humble, hardworking, and faith-filled. Raised during the Great Depression, these were fire-tried characteristics and were always quietly on display for the perceptive. Not ones to talk about themselves, they lived as people of hope. Humble but positive in outlook, they shared what they had generously, even sacrificially, and that included tithing to their local church. They did so while raising six children, on a public-school custodian's salary. Talk about living, influenced by hope!

I observed that the hope of my parents was anchored in their faith and the belief that God was a loving God who had their best interests in mind. The Jewish prophet Jeremiah, speaking on behalf of his God, captures this sentiment, "I know well the plans I have in mind for you, plans for your welfare, not for woe, plans to give you a future full of hope."

Whether by nature, nurture, or a combination thereof, hope in a good future has served as a cornerstone to my outlook on life.

Patience and Perseverance

Like any child, I had plenty of things that I wanted, and I wanted them immediately. I would often complain impatiently to my mother. As would many children, I would moan to my mother that my birthday (and its presents!) was taking forever to arrive. She would counsel me with the oft-repeated words, "Martin, pray for patience and perseverance." I would object to her suggestion! I was exasperated and had little appreciation for the value of waiting for my life's circumstances to unfold over time.

The very notion of time was irritating. I felt frustrated by it. Time was an obstacle to whatever I hoped for. Time always took so long! Gradually I learned over the course of time through experiences and reflection that my mother's words were all so wise.

Hope requires waiting and watching for that which we desire. This indeed necessitates that we develop patience and perseverance. The realization or fulfilment of our desire may not unfold as imagined while we wait and watch with hope. The journey that hope takes us on may be much better than envisioned! This challenges us to lean into That-Which-We-Cannot-Fully-Understand. Trust. Surrender. Await.

The New Beginning

When I was 19 years old, I attended a spiritual-oriented meeting on a college campus. It was a season in my life during which I was struggling intensely within myself. I was questioning, reconsidering my beliefs, searching for meaning, for purpose. I was sitting in the back, literally the last row of this gathering of 100 or so, distractedly listening to a graduate student describe a mission trip from which he had recently returned. As he shared his experience, he quoted a sentence that Jesus reportedly spoke…

"To whom much has been given, much will be expected."

Suddenly, time stood still. Those words felt like a hammer hitting my chest. It took the wind out of me. I struggled to breathe.

There, in the back of this room, unknown to those around me, the course of my life was shifting tracks. I sat, overwhelmed.

I had made a mess of my life the prior two years. I had lost interest in two of my passions – my love of learning and athletic competition. My mind and body had weakened through my abusive behaviors. I felt lost, confused, discouraged – indeed, hopeless.

I had begun to wrestle with my self-understanding, and the circumstances I had created for my life. I wanted to change. I wanted to do better. I wanted to be better. Perhaps that was why I was there that night. Perhaps it was hope that drew me there that night.

In the throes of this heart-stopping experience I silently spoke to God, as I then understood God to be.

"What could you expect from me? I am a walking disaster. I have screwed up this life. I cannot put two thoughts together. Of what use could I be?"

I could not imagine that I had anything worthwhile to give. Yet, those words…

"To whom much has been given, much will be expected"

They continued to reverberate within me.

I felt paralyzed and so inadequate to this challenge before me, within me. Then, as I drew the deepest of breaths, I replied from my heart…

"Well, whatever it is about me, that could in any way make a difference, I will try to give it my all. Have your way with me. Please help me."

This experience was a turning point. The commitment I made at that moment, there in the back row, became a profound motivating force in my life. It both set the course and served as a constant guide. It re-instilled hope within me. I became empowered by hope.

For decades I would refer to that line…

"To whom much is given, much will be expected."

It motivated me to strive to be my best self, to do my best work, to treat others with respect and kindness, to have the greatest impact possible. This single sentence framed more than four decades of my life and service. It continues to inspire me.

Soon thereafter I returned to college with newfound focus and determination. I surprised myself by the high scores I consistently received. Professional and social leadership opportunities began to present themselves. I accepted or pursued them, even with fears about my abilities to succeed. As leaders in the organizations for which I worked and volunteered began to entrust me with increasing duties, my confidence grew as my experiences unfolded. Hope was an anchor for me as my life progressed.

My Career North Star

By August of 1981, I was married. I had a daughter, with a second daughter to be born in October. I had a job I really liked. I was good at it, but I realized it did not give me a pathway to earn the kind of money I felt we would need to support our growing family.

With good advice from mentors of mine, I began an MBA program. My undergraduate degree was in theology. As someone who tended to have his "head in the clouds," an MBA was going to put my feet firmly on the ground.

As I had never taken any business classes before, I was required to take a year of prerequisite courses. The first evening class I had in the program, included eight or nine other students, several of whom were sent by a local major steel producer. The professor entered the classroom and immediately said, "Everybody, take out a piece of paper and a pen. Now write down your answer to this: 'What will be your ultimate career objective? What job do you ulti-mately want to obtain?'"

People began writing. I sat there thinking, "I don't know! Hmm... I guess something practical ..."

And then an idea "dropped" into my consciousness with a clear bing, such as a drop of water sounds as it hits the bottom of an empty metal bucket. The idea -- Vice President for University Development!

At the time I reported to that position at the midwestern univer-sity where I worked. Believe me, I had never, ever had a moment's thought previously about that position. Yet I thought, "How about that? Vice President for University Development. I could write that down." And I did.

I had a good friend who was then the development director for the university. I began asking him questions about fundraising and listening carefully to his answers and stories. As my responsibilities expanded further, I had occasional opportunities to engage in fundraising for programs and to interact with donors, including major donors.

In my next position I worked for the Diocese of Belleville, Illinois, for ten years. There I held my first full-time fundraising executive position, as its Director of Development. The diocese had 128 parishes at the time along with dozens of other nonprofit entities. Over those years I thought to myself more than once, "Well, in a diocese, this is just like being a university Vice President for Development. My position is the equivalent.

After a precious ten years – I learned so much while surrounded by thoughtful and hardworking colleagues – I took the position of Associate Vice President for University Development at Saint Louis University. During those three years I remember thinking to myself, "My boss, Tom, has such varied demands and duties, I'm really the one that oversees development. My job is just like being a Vice President for University Development."

In August of 2008, I finally reached my career North Star, the senior most position with the title, Vice Chancellor for University Advancement. From that first MBA prerequisite class in August of 1981 to this new role in August of 2008 took me 27 years. Do not be like me. I was a turtle, not a hare!

It was hope that drew me onward. Over those 27 years I had countless opportunities to practice, or at least endure, considerable patience and perseverance. Hope is nurtured and sustained in us by attributes like patience and perseverance.

But not all went smoothly over those years…

A Rough Beginning

When I was hired in 2005 by Saint Louis University to be the Associate Vice President for University Development, I was thrilled. I was hired by Dr. Steve Peterson, a truly marvelous person and consummate professional, who was serving as the interim Vice President for Advancement at the time, in addition to his primary role as the Associate Vice President of Alumni Relations and Annual Giving.

Steve told me that he was competing to be promoted to the permanent role of Vice President. I thought Steve would be a great person to work for and work with. As it turned out, the search committee had someone else in mind. They hired a fellow from Minnesota named Tom Keefe. Tom was an attorney and a seasoned, successful fundraiser. He had been an exceptional salesman earlier in his career.

I remember the night Ellen and I had dinner with Tom, at his request as he was in St. Louis house-hunting. There seemed to be a "chill in the air" during our time together. Ellen and I spoke about it afterwards, on our way home from the restaurant.

Finally, He Arrived On The Job

By this time, I had been working for several months as hard and smart as I could. His first morning at the university Tom called me into his office just before eight that morning. I was hardly seated, and looking at me sternly, he said, "You know, Martin, I specifically asked that hiring committee not to fill your position because I wanted to fill it with a person of my choosing."

I don't know what would go through your mind, but I know what went through mine, "Oh no! What am I going to do? I have been here a couple of months, and he wants to fire me? Is that what he is saying? Does he want me to resign?!"

Now, sometimes when we get in situations like that the best thing we can do is resign. Who wants to work for a supervisor who is unhappy about you being there, immediately upon arrival? But that was not what I set out to do. I was determined to succeed. I was excited about the position. I had high hopes about what I thought I could do to help the university. I was already hard at work and instituting changes. I thought, "I'm going to prove to this guy I'm the best Associate Vice President for University Development he could have ever hired," and I strove intently to make that so.

Tom appeared to soften over time towards me and seemed impressed with my efforts and the results. Are you familiar with the well-worn advice to keep your enemies closer? Not that Tom was an enemy, but it was not unusual for me to stop by his nearby office 1-3 times a day to seek his advice, fill him in on donor engagements, update him on one project or another, one staff member or another, one circumstance or another.

Gradually we formed a great working relationship. Tom liked to talk and to think out loud. I enjoyed listening to him and served as a sounding board on some occasions. He would come back from an executive meeting and tell me about them in some detail. He worked closely with university president, Father Larry Biondi, S.J., in those days, and those meetings could get "wild and wooly." I learned so much through his observations, reflections, and stories.

We would talk thoughtfully and strategize about prospective donors or facilitating relationships with current donors, and his insights and approaches sometimes were brilliant and unexpectedly creative. Hopefully, I gave him a couple ideas over those three years, too.

When I competed for the Vice Chancellor for University Advancement position at the University of Missouri-St. Louis, my understanding is that the recommendation that put me over the top was Tom Keefe's telephone conversation with Dr. Tom George, the university chancellor. I really believe that by the end of their conversation, Chancellor George would have thought himself a fool if he would have chosen otherwise.

I think it was hope that motivated me to make lemonade from the lemons I was handed through those circumstances. Did I grow, change, and stretch? My three years at Saint Louis University were like "dog years" – it felt like seven years squeezed into each year! It demanded so much from me. But I like to think that my abilities and character grew and developed as a result. It prepared me well to undertake my new role at the University of Missouri-St. Louis and do everything I could to provide effective leadership and help advance the organization among its external constituencies while increasing its funding, broader visibility, and reputation.

I do not know that I could have arrived at this new opportunity, with its challenges and opportunities, and been as effective and successful if I had not had those three apprentice-like years working for and alongside my supervisor Tom Keefe.

Hope Presses On

I retired from fulltime employment after a 40+ year career in nonprofit leadership roles. Twenty-four of those years I was privileged to serve as a senior fundraising leader for three organizations with teams that raised over $500,000,000. Now, I am nearly three years into a new chapter of my life that fills me with wonder and hope.

With gratitude, I am a founding member and serve as chairman of the board for a new NGO, World Game-Changers. Further, I am honored to serve as a board member for a new, social impact start-up, Ten10. I have high hopes for these two organizations, that both can make our world and our lives measurably better.

Hope goes before us, inspiring us to press on into the future, into the unknown, day-by-day, year-by-year. To have hope is to expect with confidence, exercising patience and perseverance along the way. A future filled with hope awaits...

www.martinleifeld.com

Sharon Griffiths (UK)

Curiosity: Why Am I Different?

According to the Cambridge Dictionary the definitions of curiosity is:

"An eager wish to know or learn about something."

As Felix Dennis writes in chapter 1 of his book: How to Get Rich ...

"For as long as you foster a willingness to learn, you will ward off sclerosis of the brain and hardening of the mental arteries. Curiosity has led many a man and woman into the valley of serious wealth"

Impact Of Curiosity For Me

Education and lifelong learning have always been one of my highest values. My chosen roles required natural curiosity, a desire to learn, creating awareness and teaching. Asking questions to get better results and meet the needs of those I worked with and served. By doing what I did, I was able to provide opportunities for tens of thousands of people to learn, as well as myself, whether it was just for interest or for gaining relevant vocational qualifications.

Over time, my income, career responsibilities and choices increased, and they have also contributed to building my wealth – not just for myself and my family, but also the legacy I will leave after I die.

By remaining curious, I was able retain the desire to learn more about what I chose to learn. A child or adult can remain curious if they have the capacity and will to do this.

Being curious can consist of one or a combination of the below:

- ❖ Asking questions to find out answers
- ❖ Reading to expand one's horizon or knowledge base
- ❖ Listening to and watching resources that answer questions

❖ Seeking out new experiences and being open to what those experiences have to offer

❖ Taking and applying different perspectives, so one can zoom in and out of situations with renewed curiosity

Curiosity As My Driver

For as long as I remember, my curiosity about what I was interested in seemed to drive me to find out answers to questions and fill my brain with answers and information. I always lived with hope, that I would find an answer that would satiate my apparent natural curiosity.

In hindsight, my 'curiosity driver' regularly persuaded me to step outside my comfort zone more times than I can ever imagine, and it kept me out of what I now call the danger zone of 'comfort and complacency'. This zone, I regularly left, but then when the adventure was over, always returned to my comfort zone for safety.

In contrast, I often wished that I were not so curious, and often when my curiosity got me in much trouble or I would experiment to find out answers myself, I would consistently push and test boundaries, whilst knowing that each little push and test could take me on a new adventure.

At times, when feeling intensely frustrated, my energy state of frustration would change to that of anger, because of the relentless appearance and deluge of questions that entered into my mind. I never understood where they came from, and no one else seemed to ask the type of questions like I did – it became a constant source of frustration.

Often when I spoke, so many times as a child and young person to others, my questions did not come out as they were intended to, or seemed silly or strange to others. I know so, because I was told, or saw others looking at each other in a certain way; or I received 'that glance' that pierced me so deep – interpreted by myself as "What is she on about?"

My Relentless Questions

Here's some of my relentless questions: I remember asking myself in childhood:

- ❖ Why am I different?
- ❖ Why do thoughts keep coming in my head and even worse never stop?
- ❖ Why don't I like me?
- ❖ Why do some adults tell us to do things that don't make sense?
- ❖ Why is five minutes NOT five minutes?
- ❖ What use am I?
- ❖ Why do adults hear me but don't listen to me?
- ❖ Does everyone have thoughts like me?

Can you relate to any of the above scenarios, from any childhood memories you have?

Sharon and Tracy: Yet More Questions…

Try to picture this image, perhaps it resonates in some way or maybe in a way you can relate to?

Two ten-year-old children having this discussion as they walked to one of their homes at the end of the school day…

- ❖ Child 1 (me): "There's something up there in the sky. Bigger than the electricity pylons."
- ❖ Child 2 (Tracy): "I know, I can see, there's big clouds"
- ❖ Child 1: "Yes, but is there something even bigger up there that makes us think our thoughts?
- ❖ Child 2: "What thoughts?"
- ❖ Child 1: "The thoughts we don't want or want to have, those loud thoughts that won't go away. Those thoughts that come into our head, that no one else thinks.
- ❖ Child 2: "Like what?"
- ❖ Child 1 "The thoughts we keep secret, because if we tell them

others might laugh at us or think we are strange and different from everyone else. I often think thoughts that are different from what others say, and I don't know why"

- ❖ Child 2: "I dunno, I just do as I'm told, saves me thinking.

Then the topic of conversation stopped as Tracy lost interest.

It was one of a few defining moments for me in my early life. A chat with another person like me, who I trusted. I'd never asked anyone these questions before. However, I didn't get many answers or maybe the answers I hoped for, but I WAS listened to.

My Vision

At the age of nine, in my summer holiday, I had a significantly profound thought. It progressed to an image in my head and I played with it until I could see, feel and almost touch a vision in my mind's eye. I decided to commit to that vision.

Fifty years later, I am now living in that image and have worked towards manifesting it as my reality.

My Promise

I remember at one point looking at the crashing sea waves then looking around and up to the sky and thinking... 'There's only me here and the birds. No one is telling me what to do, well at least not until I get back to the caravan', followed by these unforgettable words that became my non-negotiable accountable long-term life promise:

"I want to be free like this, not just for a few hours, but forever."

And so, the defining moment of that self-promise passed.

My Plan

I also thought to myself, 'If I told my ideas to anyone, I wouldn't be taken seriously and maybe I would be ridiculed'.

I then naturally decided to hatch a plan in my mind – this was it...

'I will do as I'm told for as long as I need to, but if I want to be as free as I choose to, I must work towards what I see and earn money so I can travel where I need to and do what I can, in order to be where I want to be'.

My Belief & Beliefs

I believed that only I could do it, and do it alone – just by myself, based on my limited experiences I'd had in my life. In regard to other beliefs, some have now been let go and others remaining with me, depending on whether they serve me, or those I help and serve.

Here are a few that I have either changed perspective on or removed from my belief system:

- ❖ Money had to be earnt. 'It didn't grow on trees'
- ❖ Hard work was required, in order to do my best, do well and earn money
- ❖ Being independent would require doing things for, and with myself
- ❖ Life was easier if I didn't bother others with my thoughts and ideas as there was a risk I would have to justify my thoughts or become ridiculed
- ❖ Respect for others, no matter who they were, was important, as one day they may not be here. This was clearly evident to me from an early age, and reinforced shortly afterwards at age of 10, because my little brother and my grandad died and I never saw them again
- ❖ Adults know best (apparently!)
- ❖ Skiving from hard work, was not a desired trait for when I was to start a proper job.

My Desire

In hindsight, from childhood, my desire was simply this…'I wanted to be free and live life on my terms'.

My Journey Begins

I didn't realise it at the time, but from that defining self-promise moment, I commenced the process of working towards creating the life that I wanted to live, and was already on a journey of discovery, that is still presently a work-in-progress and continually evolving.

Never, ever did I stop striving for my vision in order to narrow the gap from where I was at any point in time to where I wanted to be at some time in the future, However, with that powerful image also came the belief, thoughts and feelings that I could rarely talk to anyone about.

Working Towards This Vision

My approach for five decades involved some really key elements for success. Over time, with practice, application was undertaken with greater awareness

a) Continual planning with connection: In my own unique simple way, the way, initially as a naive nine-year-old is able to. In fact, for 50 years, I continually planned, reviewed with consistency to enable me to work towards the goal I held in my mind's eye. The "HOPE" that I had for success was translated in my plan

b) Compounding continual and consistent massive action: I consistently took intentional, impactful and meaningful action steps, aiming to narrow the gap from where I was at any point in time to the desired destination. My goal became that of compounding my results and manifesting what I saw in my mind's eye. I worked towards connecting the points in space, time and my mind space. So many steps, lots of little ones and some big ones. There were probably tens of thousands of steps taken. Probably more steps backward than forward at times. This led to my adapting the action plan and taking actions, aiming to ensure that I was focused on who I needed to work with, to achieve my goals

c) Commitment: I committed to focusing on my end goal, irrespective of changing circumstances, including those outside of my control. Problem-solving of challenges relatively larger than previously experienced, enabled me to gradually step up, respond to and solve increasingly more complex problems – both alone, and with others I worked with

d) Clarity: As I grew older, maintaining a state of clarity was often one of my greatest challenges to overcome, especially when feeling overwhelmed, due to allowing more and more into my life to increase the number of things that I could do and fit into my life. This became a rather habitual and addictive action, and I somehow derived pleasure from doing and achieving a lot of things. On the flip-side, I continually surrounded myself with distractions that began to contribute to much chaos in my life. Over time, I developed increasing knowledge and a wide range of skills that enabled me to understand and act within my identified roles, more easily step in and out of situations, reframe where I was, what I was choosing to do in different situations, and broaden my perspective to approaching any situation I was faced with

e) Compassion: Encompassing self-compassion, with self-awareness. In the last few years, I began to realise and accept that I was on my own Heroine's journey. Metaphorically, rescuing myself from a lifelong painful ongoing lifelong experience of 'UNANSWERED QUESTIONS AND INTENSE CURIOSITY'.

In the last nine months, it became increasingly apparent to me that the costs experienced, whether counted or not, were not just financial but also were immeasurable in terms of time lost (months and years); relationships not evolving as they could have potentially evolved; the physical and emotional pain felt throughout, and the tears cried when I chose to let them fall.

By investing my resources time, money (£0000's), energy) into a variety of very focused personal development learning strategies that included specific chosen mentorship, mastermind and accountability programmes. I began to replace the thoughts, and feelings in my headspace of:

❖ beating myself up
❖ feeling 'not worth it'
❖ feeling 'not good enough'
❖ feeling like 'an imposter'

Why Am I Different?

As a child, whenever asked myself that question, I began to increasingly dislike myself. I only knew what I knew – there wasn't a 'Mr Google' to help me, and I certainly didn't practise self-kindness, despite achieving many meaningful successes.

In my 'headspace', I increasingly focused on hiding what I didn't want to be seen, and on many occasions, I felt that I didn't deserve or wasn't worthy of the successes that I achieved. I knew that I worked hard to achieve them, but knowing and believing are two different things completely.

As a consequence, I entered a vicious circle throughout my life, which resulted in:

❖ feeling like an imposter in a body, I didn't really want to be

❖ being controlled by a mind that wasn't in alignment with me

It is really only in the last few years, have I increasingly – and with greater intensity of curiosity – worked with myself and others to challenge and unload the fears and beliefs that did not serve me.

My quest to understand the value of my uniqueness – and to answer that continual question

'Why am I different?' – has taken me on a journey deep within. An unexpected rewarding journey, one that was required in order for me to move forward as I do now, and to honestly say when I choose to.

Discoveries Along The Way

Here are a few of my discoveries that I share with you, perhaps you are aware, maybe not, but if just one of them adds value to your life, then how great is that?

Being different, is part of the survival of the human race. If we were all the same, at some point, everyone would be wiped-out, because the same weaknesses would be under attack, until destruction. I never really knew as a child – and I never really thought of it until relatively recently – that each person's genetic blueprint is different; as are their interests, talents, traits experiences, beliefs, emotions, weaknesses, values and their inner genius.

Is it fair to say that as humans, we all experience:

- ❖ a unique life journey and personality – initially beginning in childhood, (maybe in the womb) – that beautifully evolves over time
- ❖ an inner world (thoughts, feelings and emotions) and outer world (actions, habits and results/ outcomes) that are totally unique to us as individuals

Application

With awareness, I can be responsible for my actions if I choose to, without negative thought. I can truly be my own heroine and that no one would probably be as interested in me, as myself.

I have always enjoyed making a positive difference to people's lives – maximizing their potential and achieving their goals; narrowing their gap from where they are and where they want to be.

To do this, I always have utilised my curiosity, through listening and questioning. The questions I ask get to the heart of the matter and empower those I help. I call them my 'Super Power Tools', and combine them with the varied range of skills and expertise developed in my career including teaching, training, careers guidance, coaching, mentoring and through a process and a system of bespoke connection.

The outcomes of this powerful catalytic connection process enables people:

- ❖ to save time and money
- ❖ short cut the trust building process
- ❖ achieve more with others than alone or with those who may not be suited to them.

Music to my ears, is when I hear these immortal words, from others…

"I see an opportunity for connection, can you connect me with so-and-so?"

I know that this action is the most positive powerful thing I could ever do to help some people, because I don't just positively impact on one person; there is then the potential knock-on effect of others co-creating, and so the ripple effect is infinite – just like dropping a pebble in the pond.

Consider me like that lighthouse standing proud, shining my light to provide lightness within darkness, or that guiding light at the end of a dark tunnel. What a joy and privilege it is, to give myself the permission to embrace and celebrate my differences each day.

My final message to the world, is this…

Maybe you feel you are so different to the rest of the world, possible even in a way where you feel like an outcast at times? Whatever the case, really accept and celebrate the amazing, beautiful gift, that is uniquely YOU, and never let anyone dim your light – keep shining and radiating with childlike curiosity…

In your opinion, what's the most positive, powerful thing you could ever say to someone, or even yourself?

www.SharonGriffiths.com

Jephias Mundondo (Zimbabwe)

Finding My Life's Purpose

It is rather interesting and amazing that all human beings come into this world without any knowledge of what they have to do and why they even came here. The individual human purpose remains hidden and only a few manage to find it.

In manufacturing, even the smallest gadget has an instruction manual, but unfortunately in the case of life – important as it is – when you are born there is no such manual to follow.

This becomes a challenge to many people, and they end up with life directing what they do and never get to discover their purpose rather than directing their own lives and making it happen.

The worst thing is living other people's lives through copying and imitating or because you are trying to meet others' expectations, yet the real you will be there somewhere within, wondering what is really going on.

This is going to be a story of my journey from day one to where I am now. As I write, I call it my interesting journey. In this narration, I will be looking at how I found myself, and how I ended up finding my life purpose.

There was no manual and no signposts to my purpose. I could have followed them if they were available, and you could say how I got to where I am now was just by coincidence. However, I did manage to find my passion and purpose…

From the time you are born, you really do not know who you are or who you can be; your capacity or even your purpose for being or existing. The spark and the whispers may sometimes be seen or heard but most of the time, nothing really shows you which direction your life is meant to take.

You grow up just looking at people around you, your siblings, friends, parents, teachers and other influential people and from their experience you are also influenced and sometimes advised, and from there you become what you end up being.

When I look back, I could have unknowingly influenced my brothers, sisters and other children in the village, and subsequently my own children as well. In the process of admiring someone and following in their footsteps it hinders many from finding their own life purpose.

Being in the same situation I admired the older boys and girls in our village, got advice from my parents, uncles and aunts.

The question I asked myself is 'Who really knows where you are meant to be going, what is your real calling and purpose in life?'

After appearing and being born into the third world, my port of arrival was Masvingo a small town in Zimbabwe. It was so exciting going to school and I reached a level where I could take a course so that I could find employment. Being educated was the number one value within our family and community and I couldn't have dodged that.

My father wanted me to be a handyman, specialising in household electrical work. I never liked it but at the time I had no choice or other option either. After training I got a job, but was not happy in it.

The only good thing was that I was earning some money. I did not know my life purpose yet so there was no thought of me saying to myself 'really why am I doing this instead of something else'. I did not know what that something else was.

I changed my job and went into law enforcement. That was even worse except I enjoyed the training, parade drills, helicopter drills, firing guns and the different life experiences. It was funny – rather than purposeful – and was more of an adventure than a career.

Subconsciously I was still looking for the real thing; unfortunately, it was something that I did not even know. After three years I left law enforcement and decided to go into agricultural management. The training was great, and I really enjoyed working with animals and ended up managing cattle and wild life ranging operations.

It was a good experience and was interesting. I enjoyed it and got a few 'Cattleman of the Year' awards for the company which I was working for. It was during that phase when someone whispered to me about my life purpose.

Christie Angus was my senior and when he called me to his office I thought it was the usual feedback on operations and the planning of our activities.

He sat me down in a way which he had never done before. He said he was going to tell me something which could be a bit disheartening and offered his apology before he said:

"Jephias you are not an Agriculturist, you are doing the wrong job. You are supposed to be working with people."

I looked at his face and I saw his genuineness and saw an honest man saying something that he had been sent from the Universe to say.

I was a bit stunned as that year I had won the 'Provincial Cattleman of the Year' award. How can such an achiever and a champion be in the wrong job?

I walked out of Christie's office and went back to my office. I couldn't concentrate on my work and decided to go home for an early lunch. I locked myself in my bedroom and started asking myself various questions.

What did Christie really mean? Doesn't he like me? Does he want to push me out of this great organisation where I have done so well? Is he okay in his head or was he drunk?

It's so interesting that when your purpose is revealed to you it does not initially make any sense as you will be holding onto what you are doing at that time because it feels familiar and in your comfort zone.

This is especially so when you do not know what your life purpose is meant to be. The question of wanting to know if there was anything better than what I was doing never came in play.

This could have been due to self-doubt and not knowing how far one can grow. The fear of the unknown may also hold you hostage and you will not be courageous enough to look beyond what is in your hands at that moment.

The saying that one bird in hand is worth more than two in bush may vividly influence one to avoid trying new things.

I spent the whole week thinking over the issue and could not come up with the meaning. I asked to have a meeting with Christie. We had a meeting during which I asked him why he thought I wasn't an agriculturist and how I could move onto this new vision of his.

He said "Since you have managed the Estate which you are in charge of, you have not had a labour dispute. You respect people even those below you, love them and appreciate their service. You are a down-to-earth type of person."

'Down-to-earth, what is that?' I constantly asked myself.

He also said I should start training in any human resource management related course.

The most exciting words to me were 'Down-to-earth' – I spent the whole week saying to myself, 'Jeph, down to what, to earth?'

I started reflecting on my life to see what this down-to-earth was all about, trying to comprehend that I was able to effectively interact with all types of people, at any level.

I was able to share and listen to what people like to chat about and understood if it was important to them.

I always wanted to see myself just as human as anybody else despite being in a senior managerial position at work, but I never thought of it as my life's purpose. I said to myself if this is my down-to-earth, then Christie was right, I am down-to-earth.

As advised, I started doing my studies in Personnel Management with the then Institute of Personnel Management, which I passed really well. I was also interested in Labour Relations and Training subjects which I passed with distinctions.

The newly-acquired qualifications enabled me to be employed in senior positions as I was now more marketable. I also started being officially given Human Resource management roles. On two occasions I was head-hunted for more senior positions and started to see what Christie meant.

I continued to pursue my studying ambitions and went ahead to do a Masters' Degree in Development Management. That is when I started to realise that what was being taught in the programme resonated with my soul – helping the poor, negotiating for win-win situations, looking at things from the other person's point of view and making environmental, sustainable decisions and more.

I started recognising the down-to-earth person which I was told about and these studies strengthened the point.

Many questions came into my mind. Why had I never heard about this Development Management course before? Who was hiding it from me? Were my previous colleges not smart enough to know about that wonderful course?

Were all the people I had met in my life cycles unaware? How great things are hidden from people in life is a real mystery and how they discover what's hidden, if they do, is also another mystery.

After finding myself, I was engaged as a Chief Executive Officer (CEO), of an organisation working on HIV/ AIDS interventions in our different communities. At that time HIV was having a devastating effect in Eastern and Southern Africa. People were dying left, right and centre throughout all the communities.

There was no treatment, no knowledge about prevention and social support networks for children whose parents were dying of the virus. I had never seen children being orphaned at such a rate. It was worse than any war experienced in the region.

With all my heart, I served – working long hours, going through the pain of death, of losing parents, sisters, brothers and friends and knowing more were going to perish with no treatment. It was like millions of people falling into a bottomless pit with no immediate solution.

My heart felt the pain and at times I would close my office and just sit there in tears as I asked myself questions like 'God what should I do to make the biggest impact which will save your people'.

Surprisingly, I was so energetic and had all the enthusiasm needed to serve and save my community.

As if HIV was not enough, the economic situation in the country was also melting down. This worsened the suffering for the infected and orphaned children. It was only later that treatment was accessed mainly through funding partners from Europe, United Kingdom and America.

After 10 years, I felt I had completed my calling and took an early retirement. This was the Agriculturalist who was told by someone to leave growing maize and breeding cattle and move onto working with people.

The level of satisfaction when I retired was so great. I really felt I had achieved what very few people would have been able to do in 10 years.

I felt I had answered my call when I was needed to serve. I felt this was going to be a life honour I would carry throughout the rest of my life and my heart was filled with joy. I felt I had found my purpose and fulfilled it.

From answering one calling I felt the urge to answer another calling; while serving as the CEO of the Family AIDS Caring Trust I was about to go for my early retirement and the thought of becoming a Life Coach came in from nowhere.

Influenced by a Life Coach who trained us when I was a Board Member of the Regional AIDS Training Network, I just decided to train as a Life Coach.

Another surprise, what was this Life Coaching thing? I had never heard about it throughout my life. It was the same surprise I had when I ended up doing development work. Where was this precious knowledge hiding? Here I was learning the things I felt I should have learned when I was in school.

I knew of a Soccer Coach and had been one before, but a Life Coach was a new animal in my world. The training changed me, and I gained far more in my own life than just becoming a certified Life Coach.

My mind was stretched to levels I never thought existed in this world. Learning about how to use resources, set goals, milestones and essential action steps towards achieving your goals; learning about what beliefs are and how to break down negative beliefs and change your beliefs to new empowering positive ones and how to adopt the values you want.

I also learnt about uncovering the hidden rules you set for yourself, projection and effective communication, responsibility and the true meaning of life. How not to be judgemental, how to be more creative and understanding, how the human mind works and how we create our realities through our thinking.

Just changing my thinking changed my life. Having grown up in both African Traditional and Christianity religions where if something goes wrong something or someone else was causing it. Guys like Satan, demons, the guy next door and even ancestors were always the ones to blame for any failures in life.

I had never previously known or believed that my thoughts created my reality or that you become what you think all day long. If things didn't go well I used to think it could be because you are just unlucky.

I hadn't heard of the Law of Attraction, really how in the world can I attract my own happiness, attract wealth; even attract good friends and good fortune?

The advantages of positive thinking against the disadvantages of negative thinking started to build a castle in my mind and being positive became one of my new characteristics which I've carried forward to this day. What a shift it was! The challenges were to live that life, to teach that life and to train more Life Coaches in my community.

I started getting into reading books which had all the wisdom I have been deprived of not knowing. Books like Your Erroneous Zones, Viruses of the Mind, The Power of Positive Thinking, Ask and Its Given, Peace is the Way, Unlimited Power, Wishes Fulfilled, Inspired Destiny and many others.

I started investing in developing my mind and understanding how to get what you want in life. The interest of reading generated a hunger to also write and I wrote articles in the local weekly paper for two and half years.

My amazing journey from that farmer I used to be to this Life Coach and Life Coach trainer that I now am, was full of interesting experiences (despite not even knowing where I was supposed to be going). It was more about following the wind.

The shift from an electrician to working with cattle and wild animals to working with people still surprises me and many others. The shift from who I was and who I am, with all the wisdom and still equipping myself to gain even more wisdom makes me look back and ask myself how I really got to be where I am now and who I am now.

My journey to my life purpose was more from less awareness to enlightenment to who I am. After coaching people and seeing them also be successful on the journey to finding their life purpose, moving from doubting to knowing; I'm now really aware of my life purpose and where I was coming to after all these years.

It was to share this wisdom, to change lives, to help people awaken to new thinking, to empower people to realise their full potential and know that this life is full of possibilities – and hope!

WOW: You don't know what you don't know – so forgive yourself your mistakes as you progress along the exciting path of discovery

Tony Courtney Brown (UK)

Despite The Doom & Gloom, Hope Offers Light

Humans have been tribal in nature since the beginning of time. They have been based on geographical location, appearance, philosophy, ideology and beliefs, and race. Society then subdivides us into various social strata which may be formalised through caste systems, or less formal through class systems. It extends to support of sports teams, especially football in the UK and Europe, Apple vs Android, car manufacturers, and Instagram/ Tik Tok 'influencers'.

This is in addition to the ongoing divisions between: young vs old; left vs right; north vs south; men vs women vs trans; black vs white; rich vs poor… pick a side!

The past year has opened up new divisions: masks vs anti-masks; furloughed on salaries vs independent business owners struggling to survive, vaxxers vs anti-vaxxers, and lockdown vs anti-lockdown. These latter ones have the potential to divide us still further with the proposed vaccine passports which would effectively create a two-tier society. This would divide those who are able to participate more fully in society from those who may not with regard to communal events, pubs, and restaurants (initially), international travel, and other as yet unspecified restrictions.

From the perspective of maintaining order and compliance, this is very effective in that the population will implement the policies handed down and police themselves through shaming those who go against the narrative through restricting access and social pressure. This is aided by the greater weapon in the armoury – fear.

This is maintained and ramped up through a communications strategy which includes daily televised announcements from our leaders and experts which inform us of the dire situation we are in, the progress they are making on our behalf, and the difficulty of providing a certain solution. We are told of the importance of following the rules as a way back to 'normality', and the dangers of not doing so which will risk everyone's safety.

This is reinforced by the media with their daily repetition of the same narrative. Interestingly during this period, there appears to be less of a division between the 'right' and 'left' wing press, the message is the same. The people are then left to support or rail against this and express their views on social media. However, if those views are not 'acceptable', they are censored and deleted. This raises the question of who deletes these and why? Who gave them the right to do this? Did we elect them?

With regard to the regular media, they appear to be missing reporting on some of the important issues arising from the current situation. Conspicuously absent among the daily reported deaths are the suicides which are increasing. Also, largely absent is the fact that 3 million people have been excluded from receiving any form of income for over a year because they fall between the cracks in both/either the welfare, or business support systems. When this has been highlighted, the response has been that a lot of money has been spent supporting people through the crisis… but no help for the 'excluded' groups.

Other stories which are not accurately or proportionately represented include: domestic violence, use of food banks, loneliness, stress, overwhelm and depression, all of which have risen hugely. Children's education has suffered with untold effects on child development, and anxiety in young people with uncertain futures. This is compounded by forcing children to wear masks, preventing oxygen from reaching their developing brains. Add to this the fear that they have of being too close to each other, and relatives (hug granny and kill her), and the overload of toxic negative messages and imagery becomes too much. This increases stress and it is well known that the brain is far less capable of learning under these conditions.

The lack of the earth's resources is trumpeted as though we are in a global closing down sale and that if we do not grab certain things now, we will be the worse for it. Also, if someone else has it, it means we must go without and vice-versa. This ranges from toilet rolls and hand sanitiser, to vaccines which are being 'hoarded' by some countries at the expense of others. Again, this ramping up of 'Fear Of Missing Out' (FOMO), is designed to keep people worried and permanently stressed. This inevitable has a detrimental effect on our immune systems.

Recently I saw a post which I thought was quite interesting. It read as follows:

> 'Everything the government is doing right now is designed to make you fat, weak, stupid, depressed, lazy and reliant on the crumbs they wipe off their plates. Health replaced by pharmaceuticals. Education replaced by programming. Hard work replaced by handouts'.

Some might think this goes too far, others may think it does not go far enough. Whatever your views on this, does this mean that we are unable to work together to improve things?

One of the things that is becoming clearer during this situation, is the need for us to take more control of our personal health. For instance, particular conditions have been found to exacerbate the effects of and predisposition towards the contracting Covid. Obesity is one of the underlying factors in addition to age. In the US, over 73% of adults are overweight or obese. Of these, 42% are obese, and 10% severely obese (CDC).

In the UK, 63% are overweight, with 26% being obese. These figures indicate that prevalence of obesity is in the most deprived areas.

The prevailing 'pill for an ill' approach has led to high levels of dependence and addiction, in particular opioids relating to physical and mental health. Approximately 2.1 million Americans have an opioid use disorder. Between the years of 2006 to 2016, doctors in the US prescribed 200,000,000 opioid prescriptions every year (Statistics on Addiction in America).

In the UK, 5.5 million people every day take pills for mental and physical pain. All these come at a cost. They have side effects, they may have adverse effects on the body, they are addictive both physically and psychologically. The side effects may create other problems which lead to the prescription of further medication. Often the cumulative impact of these is not known, especially over a long period of time, but they do impact on gut flora and brain functioning… and what about our immune system?

The above are often accompanied by the drinking of alcohol, smoking, poor diet, and lack of exercise. Is it any wonder we are sick?

Now let's consider food production. Over the years, farming methods have become more intensive, having an impact on animals, crops, and soil fertility. In the area of animal husbandry, battery farming has led to unacceptable conditions resulting in disease. This has been 'controlled' by the administration of antibiotics which we then eat 'second-hand'. Animals are also genetically modified to make them bigger and grow faster. A few years ago in the US while waiting for our main course of pizza, we were offered a starter of chicken wings which we accepted. We were however shocked to be served chicken wings which were the size of turkey drumsticks. On the other hand, on a trip to Sri Lanka the following year, the chickens and cows looked positively emaciated. This begs the question, just what are we putting into our bodies and what is it doing to us?

Intensive farming methods have depleted soil fertility to the point where the crops and vegetables grown have less nutrients and are covered in pesticides which we then ingest. The cumulative effect of all this is an increase in allergies and toxic overload which our bodies are then ill-equipped to deal with. This creates inflammation, and ultimately illness.

Not so many years ago, we were told by the government that petrol was 'bad' and that we should all be transferring to diesel cars as they were better for the environment. Now, extra taxes are levied on diesel cars which we are now told are 'bad and dirty'. Many manufacturers have stopped production of these and in UK no more petrol or diesel cars will be produced after 2030 as both are harmful to the environment, and the answer we are told is electric cars.

To understand exactly what is going on here, we need to look at the source of the respective fuels. Oil has historically been supplied to a large extent by wealthy Middle Eastern countries who are able to impact world economies by adjusting the price and flow of oil to their own advantage. Things have now changed as their supplies are running out. Oil is also becoming more expensive to produce to the point it will not make economic sense.

Electric cars, conversely, will be a more economic option long-term. One of the main components are lithium batteries which are made from cobalt. At the moment, the world's largest producer of this is the Democratic Republic of Congo. Here, it is mined cheaply (there is controversy over the use of child labour), with the main mining company being Swiss owned – lower labour and production costs… better for the environment. There are however risks with its extraction including dust which is linked to respiratory disease. Congo currently produces two-thirds of the world's supply. This is linked to other leaps in technology such as driverless electric cars which will have implications for car ownership in the longer term, and opportunities for global corporations such as car rental firms whose stock is currently lying idle. Will this lead to a sharing of the wealth between the Congolese and the Swiss? Hmm…don't hold your breath.

So, those are some of the challenges facing us as a species, what hope is there?

Firstly, we need to become aware of false narratives, triggering of emotions and the division which is being constantly stoked to stop us getting together to make things better. We have to become aware of our other selves, our spiritual selves which are getting lost in all the cacophony of noise and distraction which is designed to keep us focused on fear and the negative. One way of doing this is to have a regular mental detox through turning off all devices, meditating, communing with nature and animals. Avoiding the 'news' and its harmful repetition of stressful, fear-inducing messages.

Mostly, we need to take personal responsibility and control of our physical, mental, emotional, spiritual, and financial health. To do this we have to educate ourselves on the dominant systems that run our society and decide whether it serves us.

Is the education system fit for purpose? Does the Care system work? How can we stop ourselves from being continuously divided through every conceivable means and find common ground to work together? This is going to be a monumental challenge as it involves compromise rather than constantly waging tribal war. There are aspects of our current system which actively work against us, that we need to change or disengage from.

One of the main casualties has been our ability to empathise which was so positive at the beginning, but constant 'noise' has demanded that we turn on each other and find the 'others' who are responsible for preventing things from getting back to 'normal'.

The bad news is that fear is a very strong demotivator. The good news is that there are more of us than there are 'them'. When we can see possibilities other than those presented to us, when we generate them from within, we will discover just how powerful we are. However, that will mean setting aside our pride and egos to focus on the bigger prize. Since the beginning of time, tribes have managed to set aside their differences for the greater good and the time has come for us to do so again.

There is much talk at the moment about 'following the science', as if it is infallible and nothing but the 'material' exists in the world. If that were the case, it would be a pretty bleak place. We need to rediscover our faith, and that is not meant in a religious, pejorative sense, though if we do, that's ok too. The main thing is to have faith that we can overcome adversity through strength of spirit.

Persecuted people have shown us this time and again both historically, and in the present day. Nothing worth fighting for was ever achieved without effort, and now as a species we are gradually waking up to the fact in increasing numbers that this is what we do, it's what we have always done, and it's how we have survived this far, and how we will continue to evolve in future.

Facebook: @TonyCourtneyBrown

Dr. Kimberlee Woods (USA)

Leaving Normal

Back to Normal

One of the things that I hear most from people today is that they just want things to get back to normal. They want to eat in restaurants, not be afraid to travel, go to the mall, visit family, all without wearing a mask or risking being exposed or exposing others to COVID.

I haven't wanted to go back to normal for a long time because my life was never normal in the first place. I live a life based on trust, going where I am directed, living in the flow of the moment. Yes, I still do chores and grocery shopping, but I listen to spirit and experience the magick of life on a daily basis. I have worked a job where I got a paycheck in the past, but for the last seven years, my life has been an amazing adventure filled with magickal experiences!

So, going back to normal is something I do not desire. Normal for me meant mindlessness, doing the same thing day in and day out, what others said was important, what I felt obligated to do based on ideas implanted in my brain from childhood. I was disconnected from my purpose and disconnected from me.

Freedom Within

Despite the fear, it is certain that COVID has helped all of us appreciate so many things: spending time with our family, in-person conversations, hugs and physical contact, travel, and overall freedom. But the truth is, our freedom is not gone. It can only truly disappear if we give it away because freedom is something experienced within. Yes, we can experience imposed restrictions, but that doesn't take away our freedom. Not really.

The question then is: Have we given away our freedom? The answer for me is yes. I have long felt that we are enslaved as a human race. We have been lulled asleep, forgetting who we are, why we are here, and what we are meant to do. The luxuries of life kept us complacent. In that sense, COVID has been a wake-up call not only as to what is important in life, but also as to what is happening in the world.

Two Camps

Regarding COVID, you have two camps in particular: those who trust the media and the government to guide us and help us through this "dark" time to overcome a world-wide pandemic that has impacted us all *AND* those who believe that this has been a highly-coordinated event by a group of people who use fear to control the masses, gain more power and make more money.

The first group has potentially given away its freedom by trusting what it has seen with its eyes and heard with its ears. The second group has potentially given away its freedom by trusting that one man may be their savior or by believing every alternative news source as truth, reacting to the latest theory.

Right now, both camps are primarily driven by fear. The first camp is afraid that they will never get their old lives back, and the only way to go make that happen, is to comply and ensure that everyone gets the vaccine so that we can all go about business as usual. They are afraid things will never change. They are afraid that the rest of the population will not comply with the vaccine and therefore keep others at risk. They are also secretly afraid that they may have been lied to and they fear what that would mean to the potential house of cards built on a foundation of trust in the government, media and pharmaceutical companies.

The second group is made up of various people: some who never trusted the government and want to take up arms; some that would push against any authority, not matter how it presented itself, because they don't like any freedom being stripped away; some who see this as the end of times, the apocalypse; and some who see the involvement of dark forces and strive to bring in the light. But there is still fear (the opposite of hope). Fear that free-doms can be taken away, that we will be forced to live in encamp-ments and take the vaccine (actually multiple vaccines) in order to travel or work or purchase food. Fear that we have been duped, lied to, by a group that owns the media, the pharmaceutical companies, and have the ability to pull the purse strings in Washington.

Living In Fear

The majority of our planet is living in fear, thinking thoughts of fear, wanting others to change their behavior so that they won't have to feel fear. But thoughts create. Our intolerance and hate language create. Our labels create. To move out of this fear, we have to recognize that our freedom does not lie in what another does or does not do for us. It does not lie in whether someone chooses to wear a mask or not, whether someone chooses to take a vaccine or not. The freedom we seek lies within us. And the only way to reach that freedom and move out of this fear is love.

This love is why Nelson Mandela could sit in a jail cell for over 20 years and still feel free. No one could take that from him. He did not hold on to resentment. He remembered who he is and why he was there. He didn't complain or blame. He loved himself and those who persecuted him.

Respecting Other Perspectives

Part of realizing and owning our freedom within, is recognizing that we have choice. You are free to wear a mask and free to not wear a mask. If you try to take that freedom away from another, you step outside of love. And if someone chooses to wear a mask, that ought to be respected. And vice-versa. They have their reasons. But we are living in a polarized time, where everything seems to be black or white for people.

I recently posted something on social media from Robert F. Kennedy, Jr. about the vaccine, and people were livid. He, and by association I, was irresponsible, ignorant, dangerous, a conspiracy theorist, and a nut job. Since when is it "normal" to call each other names, judge another's journey or perspective? And these were my friends.

I began to wonder what would drive people to do this, people that I love? Certainly, mainstream media backs up their perspective. So, I asked, "Aren't you concerned that you never hear another perspective?" There was no answer. We used to live in a time when you could read another perspective in the newspaper or online. But those days are over. Doctors are fired if they speak out. Their licenses are threatened if they do not comply. Those who have been on the frontlines in the CDC or vaccination creation and shared concerns were fired or suddenly, unexpectedly died.

As an example: A group of friends were going to get together for an event. One person wanted to require that everyone wear masks out of respect for those who might be immuno-compromised. Another group member spoke up saying that she felt to wear the mask would lower her own immune system by 20% (articles back that up), and that she did not want to do that. People went back and forth, desiring to be heard. Who was right? Does it matter? They both were right. The real question was: how can we come together in love and respect for one another?

I am actually part of a group of spiritual people that can see past the physical world, and that has been highly-trained in the history of our planet. I know the galactic wars that we have engaged in, how many times we have lost, and what price we have paid each time. We are in another war now. Not a war that people can even see with their own two eyes, but one that goes beyond masks, and vaccines, and "normal life." And winning this war means that we have to wake up, to go beyond the physical world as we know it, to remember why we are here, and believe it or not, to live our life purpose to the fullest.

It is easy to become afraid, to feel helpless, like there is nothing we can do. It is easy to point a finger, to blame, and get angry. It is easy to want others to fix things or comply so that we feel better. But if we want to evolve beyond our current circumstances, we must approach them differently.

In this past year, I have discovered a few ways to move beyond the current circumstances and approach this differently:

❖ **Recognize The Spiritual Intent:** Even if there has been nefarious intent regarding COVID or the vaccine, there is a higher spiritual principle at work that is helping us to evolve. We are on the precipice of moving from one paradigm to another. We are trying to do this while maintaining our physical bodies, a feat, I have come to understand, that has not occurred before in our universe. This requires us to upshift our DNA, to develop sensitivities and not reactivities to foods and our environment. And the global phenomenon of COVID, as well as the vaccine, is helping us do this.

❖ **See Beyond The Physical.** I get it. This sounds crazy. However, we all have the capacity to see the other realms. It is a muscle that has atrophied and needs to be built once again. This requires spiritual work and a desire to see beyond what is presented, what you can touch or understand through trained reasoning. Have you ever heard the saying, "There is more going on than meets the eye"? Well, there is.

❖ **Trust Within:** Nothing is as it seems. If you loved Trump: He is not the savior – we are. The Christos is within us, acting out of compassion, fully awake and aware. If you hated Trump: Look deeper. Explore border crossing and child trafficking in alternative news sources like Bitchute.com and see what you find. Be open. Have you ever thought you knew the truth to find out later that it was a lie? Only you can know the truth within, and if you are extreme on one side, there is more to explore. There is always truth buried in the lies, and there are always lies buried in the truth. Filter it out. Don't judge. Which brings me to the next point.

❖ **Neutral Perspective Of The Cosmic Eye:** One thing all the masters have in common, is letting go of all expectations and judgments and exercising a neutral perspective. It allows you to step back and respond rather than react. It allows you to see from every perspective with love for self and others, without judging how it "should" be. If you are holding on tightly to something, you have an expectation. Let it go. And if you can't, ask yourself why? What is being threatened? What are you afraid you will lose?

❖ **Love One Another**: All we need is love. If we had this, the world would be the place we want it to be. If we loved ourselves, we wouldn't need to defend our perspectives; moreover, we wouldn't need to attack another's point of view. We wouldn't wait for someone else to make us safe and create the world we desire. We would do it right now. Through love.

Love and hope can transform our reality into that magickal adventure.

www.MysticalAwakeningsInc.com

www.School-MysticalArts.com

John 'Smudger' Smith (UK)

Family, Forest And Froth

I was born and bred in inner-city Nottingham, England in the late 1940's as part of a large family. I started school in the early 50s and spent the rest of my life being judged and labelled by 'better' people than me; often wondering about the Good Samaritan and that old saying 'all that glitters is not gold'. So perhaps the opposite is true and all that doesn't glitter may be gold?

As someone that has been in the 'system' for the vast majority of my (almost) three-score & ten years, I am left to conclude there have been three very powerful and consistent influences – family, Nottingham Forest Football Club and booze – that have combined to provide me with pleasure and pain in equal amounts!

Recalling my first day at school, my teacher took me into the cloakroom and said…

"Now then, this is your coat peg; where you will keep your coat and PE bag."

I still remember the startled look of horror and disgust as I – although only about 6 years old – retorted:

"I don't want a coat peg, cos I ain't ****ing stopping!"

Whilst I cringe now at my crude response, this was normal for me at the time; my up-bringing was based upon nothing more than raw, brutal survival.

At play time that morning, I escaped to visit a nearby pond where two swans were gracefully residing. Over a period of time, the swans got to know and trust me, and I used to feed them on bread that I'd pinched from the Tuck Shop.

This pond became a haven for me; I'd paddle in it and pretend I was an Indian and I would kill all the cowboys I could (I wanted to be an Indian because all the other kids always wanted to be cowboys!).

Then in the afternoon, I'd make my way home and pretend I'd been to school all day; escaping the wrath of my Dad who would invariably be asleep upstairs – sleeping off the booze.

I remembering him once saying he was like Robin Hood – he stole from the rich and gave to the poor. Even in my infancy, I wasn't convinced that his motives were entirely selfless!

Once, he broke into a stocking factory and nicked thousands & thousands of pairs of them; resulting in practically every woman in Nottingham having enough of the damn things to last her months.

My Mam said my older brothers were out of control, so she had them sent away to children's homes. I lived with my grand-mother and I once asked where Mam went all day and all night; she simply replied, "You'll understand when you're older."

Because Dad was always in and out of prison, we didn't have much money, so I started stealing. At first, it was just small things from shops; then I hit on a brainwave. About three streets away from our house, was a coal yard, so I decided I could follow my Dad's Robin Hood example and supply the entire neighbourhood at a cheaper rate.

At first it was okay, then it seemed like hard work – I needed an easier enterprise! My conditioning for stealing was ever-growing; I know now I was creating a certain belief system around my identity and this was galvanised even further, by a simple need to survive. I progressed onto bigger things like breaking into shops and offices.

By now, the money was starting to come in. I would wait for my gran to go to sleep and then, I would deposit some of my ill-gotten gains into her purse. I think she'd rumbled me though because she'd often defiantly assert, "One day, you'll end up in Bagthorpe" (Nottingham Prison).

One morning, my Mam said I could go to Juvenile Court with her to see one of my brothers. I was about nine years old at the time and was really excited at the prospect. When we were there, a policeman told me it would be alright for me to go downstairs to the cells and visit my brother.

I jumped at the chance, but my elation soon turned to despair as the copper said to me, "I don't think you understand son, you are being sent away as well; because your Mam doesn't want you – and besides, you keep missing school! I felt frightened and betrayed like never before.

I got to the children's home about tea-time and I can still vividly recall with delight, my first meal of egg, chips & peas; with jelly for afters. I thought this is posh, cos I've never had jelly before.

I was moved from home to home and never found love or happiness anywhere. When I was about 13, me and some mates stole 24,000 cigarettes; we each carried 6,000 apiece – in large cardboard boxes – back to Nottingham on the bus.

As we proceeded to get rid of the stash, someone grassed on us, so I decided to go on the run to Chesterfield (a nearby area). I headed for a pub where all the villains and prostitutes used to frequent; I was 'advised' I'd be safe there.

The woman that ran the pub was an old-ish lady and she used to take 'clients' upstairs. I disgustingly recall how some of the men wanted me to watch the 'performances' and some even wanted me to join in! To me, this was all perfectly 'normal' though, because my own Mam had always carried on this way.

The men used to get me drunk and I still remember sipping my first pint of beer, through the huge frothy head at the top of the glass, thinking to myself at the time, this stuff's good – I could get addicted to it!

Eventually when I'd returned to Nottingham, Mam had left my Dad; his drinking had become even worse. Because Mam was no longer there to see to his intimate comforts, he started to molest me.

He said it would be alright so long as I never told anyone, but I instinctively knew this wasn't right, so I deliberately got caught on a job; so I'd be sent away, as far as possible from Dad.

Over the years, the crime continued, with my earlier motive of providing money for gran, long-since gone. By now, I was consumed by anger, hatred and a total lack of self-esteem. I was carrying an immense amount of toxic venom towards my parents for teaching me this way of life and setting me on the road to despair and destruction.

The realisation that my Mam was a whore, and my Dad was a nonce (child molester) caused me immense suffering let alone pain, and this self-hatred carried on well into my thirties, until a dramatic event changed my life.

I was in prison – in the middle of another sentence for burglary – when a close friend on the outside committed suicide. I totally immersed myself in victim mode, blaming myself for his death because it wouldn't have happened if I'd been there, right? Wrong!

I just wanted to die and this misery and suffering continued, turning to depression. The guilt remained with me for some time until one Sunday – out of total desperation – I attended the prison Chapel.

For the first time in my perceived miserable existence, I began to feel shame about my crimes; I cried over and over again with genuine remorse and vowed I would make amends to society, once I was free.

These formative decades of my life gave me an extremely negative perception of what family life was all about; the events that unfolded over the ensuing years, could not have been more contrasting. Family became the very glue that gave my life meaning and purpose; still with challenges though!

I first met my ex-wife Alice – who already had three children – in 1979 and the relationship progressed to the point that we had a beautiful daughter, Collette between us in 1980. Three years after this elation-filled event, Alice was raped and my responsibility as I saw it, was to protect my family and seek revenge.

I managed to find out where the cowardly scum lived and set about my task. Upon arriving at his place, I kicked the door in and stabbed him in his balls; I wanted to make sure he wouldn't rape anyone else. For this, I got a 5½-year prison sentence; whilst the rapist got three years – for 3 rapes – justice eh?

As soon as I came out in 1987, I got custody of Collette because Alice and I had split up whilst I was in prison. My daughter and I were blissfully happy although we didn't have many possessions, and I had hardly any money to support us, initially.

I managed to get painting and decorating jobs and was absolutely determined that Collette would enjoy a warm, loving and secure childhood – something I'd never had. This continued for years and my daughter has turned out to be a beautiful well-balanced soul, with two grand-kids that I worship & adore.

Later in life, I met a lady called Carol and the universe conspired to repeat itself and grant us a beautiful baby girl – Shannon. My two amazing daughters – as well as my step-children with Alice, have been a powerful force of love and I know without doubt, that they have given me a reason to live and a purpose.

As a kid, I was constantly labelled as being illiterate and was advised – on one of my juvenile detention centre 'holidays' – to find something that interested me. Consequently, I started researching all professional football clubs in England, so that I could better understand my passion around the one that I loved – Nottingham Forest FC.

Whilst in borstal, Nottingham Forest were my very reason for living – along with my beautiful daughter Collette – and I now rationalise this as creating a sense of identity; needing to be part of a tribe and belong.

In 1959, Forest reached the FA Cup Final at Wembley – every football supporters dream – and my Dad promised to take me.

However, the bastard let me down as usual, and went with all his boozing mates, without me. All was not lost though; the guy at the local fish and chip shop gave me a load of batter bits, to compensate!

Years later, fate ensured I met up with Psycho – not the Forest legend Stuart Pearce, but the creator and co-author of this book – Paul D. Lowe. I gave him that name because of his fearless attitude and his never-say-die spirit; he was unlike anyone I'd ever known, including all my borstal and prison acquaintances!

Forest wasn't the only thing we had in common – we both had serious drink addictions and we'd spend hours talking about our tortured pasts and how one day, we might enjoy a different life. I started drinking at 13 to numb the pain and suffering of my shameful existence.

As I enter the twilight of my very challenging life, my one big regret is that I missed so many years of my kids – and step-kids – upbringing. The legacy I leave though, is I managed to break the parent abuse and neglect cycle and as such, all my years of learning and paying my debts to society has meant they haven't had to – I'm so proud of them all and love them immeasurably.

WOW: Never under-estimate the power of love and hope

John Batterby (Spain)

A Successful Life Of Service

In offering an overview of my life so far – giving insights into my journey – I believe the best place to start, is to define what prosperity means to me, namely: achieving whatever goals I set out to do and being the very best I can be.

On that basis, it's fair to say I live a life of prosperity in Spain – and have done so for the past 12 years – although there have been one or two significant challenges along the way, including going to war at 16 and being involved in two divorces – as well as a massive identity crisis at the age of 41.

I was born on 13th April 1965 and bred in Sheffield – a very industrial working-class part of northern England. Although my family weren't rich by any stretch of the imagination, my two younger sisters – Claire and Louise – and me were all a happy bunch and always felt well-provided for, loved and protected.

My mother was a strict disciplinarian and worked as a secretary at a local carpet shop. Dad – whom we seldom saw as kids – was a very hard working self-employed painter & decorator and a typical 'Northerner'.

He would normally pop into the local pub for a pint after work and the only time we really saw him was when he'd come home and say nite-nite before bedtime, and during the two or three family holidays abroad that we were lucky enough to have most years.

A strong work ethic and honesty were values that were instilled in us as youngsters and these are things that I still hold close to my heart today. I suppose that's why I've never understood people with talent not having that work ethic; talent is nothing without taking the necessary action to make things happen.

That said, I was academically very lazy at school – I left with two O' levels in Physics & Cooking. I was interested in becoming a chef but wasn't sure how to achieve it. My grandfather was in the Coldstream Guards but died when my mother was nine so I think it was because of him that I also always had this idea of being in the military to fulfil a career that he wasn't able to.

My mother was worried about what I was going to do, so she made enquiries and took the initiative to organise my first interview with the Royal Navy; this took place in December 1979 with me not yet 15 years of age!

Upon leaving school on Friday 29th May 1981, I travelled from Sheffield Railway Station and less than 48 hours later to Plymouth (in the south-west of England) to begin what would become a long and distinguished Naval career. On Monday 1st June – barely three days after leaving school – there I was ready to begin training.

My first introduction to Navy life, was the barber politely – and upon reflection, sarcastically – asking me which parts of my long, curly hair I'd like to keep. Upon meticulously explain which bits were okay to cut and which bits needed styling, he duly obliged by shaving the lot off down to the bone!

I entered as a trainee chef and did six weeks' basic training and a further 6-7 months trade training; then I was posted to HMS Cochrane in Scotland.

After five years as a chef, I re-categorised to become a Royal Navy Clearance Diver – part of this trade involving EOD (Explosive Ordnance Disposal/ Bomb Disposal) – but this came after the 'small' task of being involved in the Falklands War.

The Falklands War (April 2nd –June 14th, 1982) was a military conflict between Great Britain and Argentina on the issue of sovereignty over the Falkland Islands. The British eventually surrounded the Argentine troops at the capital, Port Stanley, and forced them to surrender.

At the time, the general understanding was, that we were only going there as a 'warning' to the Argentinians; we were led to believe that – by the time we got there – it would have all blown over. Furthermore – because of my tender years – I shouldn't have even been on the ship, going into a potential conflict.

However, I sailed on HMS Brilliant from 2nd April 1982 to June 14th, 1982 and hadn't even finished my training before I was involved in the harsh realities of war.

I was the youngest member to serve in the Falklands – at 16 turning 17 – and this taught me some monumental life lessons.

At the time – in my immaturity and ignorance – I thought of it all as a game which I now realise protected me massively from experiencing the fear and trauma that many of my colleagues suffered.

At that age I thought I was invincible, although I now concede my flippant attitude towards the possibility of dying was more down to naivety than any great courageous awareness.

The reality being, I was far too young to understand the dangers; I'd comfort grown men – in their late 20's early 30's – after constantly observing them break down and cry; it was difficult for me to understand. I suppose the modern-day term would be ignorance is bliss.

With heart-wrenching casualties on both sides – the inevitable consequence of war – we lost a few guys on our ship and others got injured with shrapnel and burns.

After the trials and tribulations of the conflict, we arrived back in the UK and were given heroes' welcome which we didn't expect; there were thousands of people everywhere, fireworks going off and a real party atmosphere.

We were all allowed a phone call – I phoned my Dad because it was his birthday and announced, 'Happy Birthday Dad, we've won I'm on my way home' – he simply replied, 'Good lad'.

It was on the back of the Falklands War that I decided I wanted to be more than just a chef and do and achieve more with my life.

As someone that massively believes in the power of having a positive mindset, I would say this experience was a magnificent challenge; in later years, the reflection of the events acted as a really strong way of re-enforcing my 'have no regrets and live-for-today' attitude. Despite all the pain and suffering that war inevitably offers, I was grateful to have served.

In terms of my awareness towards pain, my life has always been black & white – obviously significantly conditioned by my years of extensive service and training within the Royal Navy; ranging from being a chef – sandwiched by the demands of Clearance Diving (there were still ¾ of a million mines from World War 2 around the British shores that needed diffusing) – and being part of a world-respected Field Gun Crew.

The Royal Navy's Field Gun competition is a contest between teams from various Royal Navy commands, in which teams of sailors compete to transport a Field Gun and its equipment over and through a series of obstacles in the shortest possible time.

In the case of Field Gun Crew, this was the highlight of my Royal Naval career. It was the ultimate thing in the navy.

Although it involved extremely hard physical training for weeks on end, it was the epitome of efficient team-working and contributed massively towards my identity of being someone that could always be relied upon and would never let anyone down.

After 25 years' my time was served; I was pensioned-off at the ripe old age of 41! Now I suppose for most people, they may think that to have been able to serve your country with distinction and then have a nice pay-off at the end, would be a great situation – it wasn't!

I became very confused about what to do each day; all certainty had been removed. I'd been part of a very regimented institution where you're so well looked after – you're fed, you're clothed, and everything is done for you.

Repetition and routine – and following disciplined orders – had become my very life for a quarter of a century and now, there I was like a rabbit caught in the headlights; not knowing what to do next.

Worse still, I felt like as if I didn't know who I was or where I was going; not only had I lost my identity, but my purpose in life too. The whole transformation process was very difficult, and I instinctively knew that – if I was to have any chance of recapturing my previous positive outlook – I needed a clean-break and new goals.

To compound things even more, I was also going through a messy divorce. Consequently, I decided to emigrate to Spain to get away from it all and re-start my life. Interesting how fate steps in and offers you some alternative paths when you need it most.

Newly-landed in Spain, it was one of the lowest times I'd had for a long time, I was mindful that I needed to get a job and was thinking 'what am I going to do?'. Then after doing a few menial things, in a roundabout way the military helped me out.

I bumped into a guy at the local pool who was an ex-Irish Ranger, he was setting up a security company, we got talking and became partners in the company.

I built upon this successful business – I've always had a keen interest in health & fitness so in 2010 I took my Personal Trainers' course and became a fully-qualified Personal Trainer.

It's amazing how you can condense a whole lifetime's very diverse experience under a few simple headings.

Having recently become aware of the power of the Learning – Loving – Legacy values, I can easily make sense of these key areas within my own brilliant service-driven voyage.

Learning – You learn something every day even if it's on the back of something bad, no matter how minimal it is. I really believe life's journey is a learning curve. Having goals and new achievements to work towards and constantly wanting to improve myself has provided me with huge benefits.

Loving – My self-love and self-belief is a product of my secure family upbringing. Because of my extensive military training – particularly in bomb disposal –you almost become a robot. I've been trained to detach myself from being too emotional – you switch yourself off and even now I'm aware that I'm still not back to being who I truly am.

Legacy – To me, this is all about being remembered for something. Yes, you've guessed it – being positive; my glass is always half-full, never half-empty and having no regrets.

I simply want to be remembered for being 'Smiling John' – sharing my attitude with people and generally, helping them the best way I can. That legacy means more to me than leaving millions of pounds, buildings, or institutions behind.

I am now very secure in my identity of being someone that will always be of good service to others; I'm certainly not a 'people-pleaser' – but I am a bit of a soft touch and do like to help people out and see them happy.

My vision is quite simple: to live a long healthy happy life; and to achieve many goals. I only wish my beloved football team – Sheffield United Football Club – manage to excel in the field of achieving goals!

Life could have been so much more difficult. I've witnessed so many of my colleagues struggle post-war and post-service career; with so many ending up homeless on the streets.

I know my values of Health, Happiness, Positivity, Loyalty and Truthfulness have been a constant source of strength and guidance for me.

WOW: Always strive to be positive – no matter how big the challenge – because it will serve you multi-fold along your journey through life

John@The-Alpha-Method.com

Paul Kelly (UK)

Hope Is Where The Heart Is

Unfortunately, most people during the course of their lives, will experience difficult and troubling times where things happen that they do not want to happen. Life has a tendency to challenge us and test our resolve and we either sink, or swim. Throughout my life, I like many have endured some difficult days, weeks and longer sustained periods of frustration, depression and suffering. One thing has always carried me through these turbulent times, though – hope.

When at my lowest, there has always been something or someone who has given me hope. Sometimes, it has been a partner, sometimes it has been sport, sometimes it has been a friend but always this little word called hope has entered the arena or my mind at just the right time. Hope and I have formed a strong bond that I believe will never leave me and hopefully, I will be able to transfer this unselfish power to you, so you can also banish your fears, and set yourself and your heart free to be your best (true) self once again.

So what does the word hope mean to you?.

For me, the word hope encompasses a feeling of small positivity. It is what inspires us as individuals to continue when challenging times enter our lives. When we have hope, we have something to cling onto, a strong belief that better times will eventually come. Whether we realise it or not, hope is a fundamental part of people's lives. Whilst we are on earth everyone is continually hoping for something to happen, whether it be a close friend recovering from cancer, or something as simple as a bus arriving on time when we are waiting unsheltered in the rain.

The word hope is a warm feeling that we attach significance to, and is closely related to our internal belief systems.

The Feeling Of Hopelessness

During times in my life, I have occasionally felt totally helpless, devoid of any positive feelings or beliefs. Some people may question how this can happen to someone who appears to be happy, full of confidence and enjoying life.

The rollercoaster of life often changes our perception of who we, what we are about, and whether we are doing the correct thing in any given situation. A fantastic, independent individual can be rocked by a sudden unexpected family bereavement to such an extent that over a period of time, they see no future and no point to carrying on their life. Such a truly, shocking and life-changing event can have a massive impact on even the strongest of individuals. Unfortunately, in life accidents happen, tragedies occur more often than we all would like them to and if we do not have the support of friends and family, as humans we can soon become overwhelmed and consumed by feelings of 'what if I were there, maybe X would not have happened to Y'.

These very real feelings and emotions can consume all our positive thoughts and totally destroy what we had previously believed. How does this happen you might ask? When we are feeling at our best, we feel almost invincible and that nothing bad can actually happen to us or our nearest and dearest. We feel like we could climb Everest with the right equipment and support team behind us. When tragedy strikes, all of our belief systems have been pulled from under our feet. Our sense of certainty in the world has been destroyed and our positive energies have disintegrated in the space of minutes.

How can we deal with these terrible feelings of hopelessness and of feeling overwhelmed? The answer to this question is as simple as it is complicated. We are all different, we all cope with different things in different ways; the key is to revert to our closest friends and the people we truly trust and who know us best. Easy for me to say, not as easy for everyone to do. I view hope as the positive alternative to hopelessness.

For me HOPE stands for the following:

Healing Our Past Emotions

By learning from experiencing times of hopelessness in our lives we can find ways to come to terms with the negative feelings associated these times of despair. In fact as we grow as individuals, we learn not to dwell on the negative happening and reframe the story in a more positive light. Experience and history shows us that if focus on the positive aspects of our life, rather than the negative, then we will be able move forward with our lives quicker.

We will have all heard the phrase that people are living in the past. As a Nottingham Forest fan, this has been labelled at me year after year. People do tend to hang on to and remember positive experiences from their past, whether it be countless trips to Wembley or comparing their present relationship unfavourably with their past one. Is this just human nature, or is it simply our brains looking to hold onto positive past outcomes to remind us that they did exist and will exist again in the future?

From my past and through my own personal life experiences, I believe that Nottingham Forest and the city of Nottingham is magic and that good things will happen to me once again.

Why Is Hope Important?

Hope is important as it allows us the belief to move from negative experiences in our lives, and helps us to strive for happiness in our future. During the course of our life, when things are not going well, it is important to have the faith, resilience and trust that things will get better in the course of time. By having a positive outlook, we can build ourselves back up little by little each day. When things get tough, it is essential not to get stuck in a negative cycle, or a rut, but to re-establish a routine that keeps things moving forward.

In my more troubled times, I did not have the awareness to set myself any goals, or do anything that I enjoyed. I drifted from one experience to another without any real plan of how I was going to kick-start my life again. Everyday seemed like a year, and it was a constant battle to survive the day, then another battle to get to sleep when night fell. I lost all faith that there were any solutions to my problems, or that life would improve again. The feeling of not wanting to burden somebody else with my problems or how I was feeling superseded the fact that I actually really wanted somebody to help me find a solution, offer me some light at the end of the tunnel. The tunnel seemed endless, and the darkness enveloped every day but looking back many of the feelings I had I could not change. Many of the things that had happened were (seemingly) not my fault, nor could I have changed them, but my not discussing them with anyone, I was actually exacerbating them and allowing them to fester and multiply like a contagious virus.

By not seeking the light at the end of the tunnel, by not believing that things would improve, I was essentially ensuring the tunnel would be continuously extended. The negative mindset that had become entrenched within me was becoming a self-fulfilling prophecy. I became happy living day-to-day, not hoping for anything except to wake up the next morning. Fortunately, I had a few things to focus on my children, my job and cricket and Nottingham Forest, and it only took one of those four things each day to keep a spark burning within me.

What Is The Power Of Hope?

As time passes, people develop qualities that they do not know they possess. A few kind words can provoke a few positive beliefs. A few positive beliefs can create a smile. A smile can create further positive thoughts and all of a sudden a gradual change in mindset can start to evolve.

Even when we at our lowest point in our lives, at rock-bottom, we can acknowledge that the only way is up, and that in itself is a more positive outlook than stating that our life is over and that we do not have a future.

Having hope gives us the strength and courage to move forward tentatively at first, which in turn can lead to an increase in confidence, which can lead to us starting to believe more positive things will eventually happen once again in our lives. As hope increases, we can, one day at a time, learn to come to terms with our past negative experiences, and times where we may have been perceived failures, and start to make plans and develop future intentions and goals of how we can rebuild our life.

After a traumatic experience in life, whether it is an illness, a family bereavement, or the breakdown of a relationship, it is important to take enough time out to heal. Depending upon the circumstances of the trauma, we can as humans need varying amounts of grieving, thinking or healing time. By taking stock of where we are currently at in our lives and evaluating our new current needs, we can begin to decide what our best source of making forward progress will be. If we dwell on what has happened we are giving the negative experience more power and energy. However, hard the situation is we must deal with the present and take the learning from the experience and reframe it with any positive slant we can.

For some people depending on how long this healing process takes, it may be necessary to seek guidance and inspiration from a bereavement counsellor, or an expert in trauma. From my own personal experiences, the longer I kept my sentiments to myself, the more they manifested and became unbearable and over-whelming to the point where my thought processes started to become irrational.

By talking to experts, I was able to unravel the complexities of my issues, dilute my problems and develop solutions to even the most difficult of situations. Sometimes it is necessary to seek help and discussion led me to find hope where at times I believed there to be none. Once hope has been restored healing can take place, plans for the future can be formed, goals can be set and living one's life begins to become more natural. I believe a problem shared is a problem halved, and two minds are more likely to solve a problem than one confused mind.

Hope Is Nothing Without Action

One of the hardest things to achieve in life, is to overcome adversity successfully. I have spoken about some of the issues we can encounter illnesses, bereavement, relationship breakdown, losing our jobs and even our homes and how – with the help of experts and our partners or friends and family – it can become easier to find solutions to our problems.

The best doctors, psychologists, counsellors and hypnothera-pists and physiotherapists can offer and show us a way to recovery but none of this will ever happen unless we take initial action. As soon as we start to take action, the words of the experts start to take on meaning and we are now able to take their calculated thoughts and processes and bring them to life. For example, A professional sportsman nearing the end of their career could suffer a serious anterior cruciate ligament knee injury. After having their surgery, they are instructed by their surgeon that in the best case scenario it maybe a year before they are able to play their beloved sport again. The surgeon also advises that although the surgery has been a success, that a total recovery will need a little luck, intensive physiotherapy sessions as well as plenty of hard work and some pain along the way. The individual now has hope, a plan of action that they need to follow strictly, and the knowledge and awareness of the timescale and the dedication needed to make a recovery. The sportsman is likely to heed the surgeon's advice and take the appropriate action to ensure they can be back playing sport as soon as they can. The same sportsman could, however, choose to ignore the surgeon's advice, not do the exercises the physio suggests, and simply hope for the best.

On a daily basis we as humans suffer and encounter obstacles; we seek out hope and advice, yet most of us do not take action – preferring to get sucked deeper and deeper into cycles of depres-sion, self-alienation and procrastination until usually we reaching a breaking point or become so desperate that someone feels the need to intervene to save us from ourselves. We can hide our true emotions from our partner, our work colleagues, our friends for years and years and say I am ok, when deep down we know that ok is not good enough and we are far from it.

In my own life it has taken me 25 years to recover from incidents from my past. I hoped that I would recover both physically and mentally much quicker than that, but although I sought help from time to time, I did not dig deep enough and merely kept scratching the surface over and over again. In my own words, I was okay, but emotionally I was never in touch with my true self. I did not take action to understand why I felt like I felt and until I was able to describe it and write about, I was suffering from it on a daily, weekly, monthly and yearly basis.

I hope that anybody who reads this story – who may be unsure about how they feel – takes positive action and asks for help to find their true self.

You can hope that you will find yourself but unless you take action you may not be able to repair or rewire your brain's thought processes. I see life simply now – less is more. Less is best.

Hope, believe, repair achieve. Do not wallow in misinformed self-pity and despair. By returning to hope and a more positive informed way of thinking, the road to a better life will start to flow. Once life begins to flow, our beliefs become visualisations and in time, turn into manifestations and we are once again able to realise our dreams.

The key to hope, is allowing love to conquer any fear that enters your mind; on your journey to becoming your better self or your new improved self. All the obstacles we overcome serve a purpose of learning that we can take on board and use powerfully to our advantage in the future. Our new-found experience of emerging from adversity shapes our ability to move forward more quickly the next time we encounter challenging times in our lives.

Please embrace the fear, let love and hope rule, and see how quickly a few people can change the world – and the lives of thousands of other people – 'simply' by giving them hope.

www.Paul-Kelly.com

Kristin Johnson (USA)

Success

Success, the Jade Elusive Sly

Success
Emma H. Liebold, Also Writing as "Otilia Schiewe," 1935

Success, the jade elusive sly,
Leads us a merry chase,
Till worn out by it all, we turn
And meet her face to face.

With lavish hands, the fickle one
Then every gift bestows,
That half the sweetness now is gone
Tis well indeed she knows,

For we have followed her so long,
Lured by her witching smile,
We left behind us all the things
We now find most worthwhile.

Success, you jade elusive sly,
Must you always withhold
The treasures at the rainbow's end
'Till we are tired and old?

This poem, composed by my great-grandmother Emma Liebold
and published under her pen name of "Otilia Schiewe," is as true
today as it was in 1935. This essay is not meant to be a discourse
on my great-grandmother's life and career as a published author
and speaker, because every person in this book no doubt has a
great-grandmother/grandfather, aunt, uncle, or grandparent who
wrote poetry or raised a family or did deeds that never made it into
the history books (or got published on the Internet.) These unrec-
ognized people may very well be unsung heroes.

Whenever a writer sees his or her work in print, it feels like a success. The scribes who appear in this book may have that feeling, although, for some of us, it's not our first publication and byline. We can show off our chapters and our names on the cover of this attractive volume. We can post about our achievements, and give our co-authors laurels, on social media.

Is that success? It depends on your definition.

"Success, The Jade Elusive Sly"

This first line hints at the *tease*, the flirtation that makes us actively seek success. What does that tease look like?

It could be the day you hit a home run in baseball or scored a winning goal in soccer as a kid. It could be standing up and making a winning argument in a mock trial for law school. It could be making money selling your products on Etsy or winning a chess game (or playing against a grandmaster, no matter the outcome.)

Whatever it is, you know it when you feel it. That sense of accomplishment. You also know when the "jade elusive sly" slips out of your reach. That doesn't mean striking out, or failing to kick the goal, or not making a single sale.

Instead, a better definition of "jade elusive sly" is having that first taste of success and wanting more. You hit the ball once and you want more – and that's the name of the game (unless you are a pitcher, and then your goal is to pitch a perfect no-hitter.)

Cynics might say that in chasing that feeling of success we're chasing a high – which rhymes with "elusive sly."

"Leads Us A Merry Chase"

"So the question that we've got to ask ourselves is what success is to us. What success is to you. Is it more money? That's fine, I've got nothing against money. Maybe it's a healthy family. Maybe it's a happy marriage. Maybe it's to help others. To be famous. To be spiritually sound. To leave the world a little bit of a better place than you found it. But continue to ask yourself that question. Now your answer may change over time, and that's fine. But do yourself this favor: whatever your answer is, don't choose anything that will jeopardize your soul." – Matthew McConaughey, Academy Award-Winning Actor, Author (view the full speech on YouTube: https://www.youtube.com/watch?v=OKJImnk-gzQ)

Who hasn't chased success? Even now, in the coronavirus pandemic era, people are still pursuing success – even if that success is just getting through the day and living life in this new reality (while, of course, staying healthy and Covid-free.) While this crisis may be unprecedented, the idea of people pursuing success during less-than-favorable, even tumultuous, times is not new. In fact, it's a story as old as human history. And your definition of success, as Matthew McConaughey observes, may change over time. But if you are going to chase success, don't choose anything that will damage your soul.

When the difficult times end, you want to be left standing with your soul intact.

When my great-grandmother composed her poem, the world was in the throes of a Great Depression that lasted from the stock market crash of 1929 until the outbreak of World War II in 1939. I have no idea if the Great Depression had any influence on the sentiments in the poem.

"Till Worn Out By It All, We Turn"

It's easy to get worn down chasing a dream, even if it happens to be the reason you get up in the morning. You can become worn out making sure your family is healthy (the pandemic has been challenging for many in that regard!) You may exhaust yourself trying to make the world a better place, or as President Theodore "Teddy" Roosevelt would have it, spend yourself in a worthy cause. And if you fail, at least you'll fail "while daring greatly," and, according to Teddy Roosevelt, never join "those cold and timid souls who neither know victory nor defeat." (Do yourself a favor and read President Roosevelt's full speech, "The Man in the Arena," at https://www.theodorerooseveltcenter.org/Learn-About-TR/TR-Encyclopedia/Culture-and-Society/Man-in-the-Arena.aspx.)

But chasing success and pursuing a dream can be exhausting. Aiming for something, even if it's just playing a perfect baseball game, is tiring. Challenging yourself to grow is tiring, especially if you're surrounded by uncertainty.

Sometimes, whether you're helping your family and friends eat healthier (and yourself in the process), speaking up in a Zoom meeting for your nonprofit group or playing that perfect game, you chase that goal so hard that achieving the goal becomes the main thing. You need your family to take their vitamin C and zinc. You need to be heard in that meeting. You need to hit a home run. Sometimes, the smallest thing becomes all-consuming. If we achieve it, we'll be happy – or so we think.

The problem is that once you've hit that home run, you enjoy the success, but then you experience a strange let-down feeling – and possibly a sense that you could have played even better. One success, no matter how small, makes you hungry for more. You yearn for bigger and better things.

Maybe you yearn to be a World Game-Changer.

But eventually, you just want a change from the game, because it's gone into extra innings. Or you can't stand the sight of your computer screen after too many Zoom meetings and classes. Surely if you take enough seminars, do all the right things, follow the training, you'll reap the rewards and get noticed, right?

Sometimes, we've had enough of the rat race, or whatever race we're running. We miss time with our family and friends. We miss the things we brushed aside in order to chase success. Then we turn back to take the long walk home.

We've all heard the adage that "Winners never quit." But sometimes, we need to turn around and adjust our course, and in so doing…

"And Meet Her Face To Face"

Plot twist! By doing the opposite of what we've been doing, we find ourselves meeting success.

Truly, "With lavish hands, the fickle one/Then every gift bestows."

The generosity looks different for everyone, but you know it when you see it. Suddenly, the universe seems like unicorns and rainbows, if only for a moment.

We get what we want – if not everything we want, then at least more than we had. But at first, we might doubt our good fortune. When I'm working hard to achieve something – in my relationships, career, health, finances, personal development, even something purely for fun – I sometimes experience a moment of "I can't believe it" when I attain it. At times I doubt every gift that success, "the fickle one," chooses to give me – which is unproductive and a waste of energy. After all, when people in our lives achieve success, most of us are happy for them, right? We don't say, "Yes, but this can't last," or, "It's too good to be true."

But then hope grows. Hope that I can do it again. That I can repeat the success in bigger and better ways. It's not just in terms of tangible rewards. For example, if I call a friend who is having a difficult time, and they're happy after the call, I hope that I do even better the next time I talk to them or get together. It's not a competition by any means. I'm not trying to be better than anyone else – only better than what I was yesterday and the day before.

This is part of the merry chase. It's also one of the ways that success operates – keeping us chasing after her. (N.B.: I am using "her" because of the language of the poem.) This isn't necessarily a bad thing. In the poem "Andrea Del Sarto," Robert Browning wrote,

"Ah, but a man's reach should exceed his grasp, or what's a heaven for?"

All this focus on success might feel a bit hollow now that we actually have met her, seen her face-to-face, even chatted with her. It's a bit of a letdown. We've built up our expectations not only to "high apple pie in the sky hopes," we've launched our hopes into orbit. Coming back down to earth is going to be difficult.

"That Half The Sweetness Now is Gone"

"After a time, you may find that having is not so pleasing a thing, after all, as wanting. It is illogical, but it is often true." – Mr. Spock (Leonard Nimoy), "Star Trek" ("Amok Time")

We get what we want – and it feels fantastic, for a time. Unicorns and rainbows abound. But then, one of several things happens:

124

- ❖ Success breeds success.
- ❖ After the success, we experience a string of failures.
- ❖ Success leaves us unsatisfied—we're addicted to it. We crave it.
- ❖ We downplay success because people feel insecure or aren't as happy for us as we think they should be.

This last phenomenon puts a damper on the sweetness, because half the enjoyment of our triumphs and treasures is sharing them with the people closest to us, and of course to our "friends" on social media. Even if that success involves sitting and meditating and achieving total inner peace for half an hour (and being able to sit still that long while keeping distracting thoughts to a minimum), you still want to share it with everyone you know.

But when you don't get the likes you expect or the reaction you expect, does that invalidate the success? Not at all! This reaction to our small or large victory is part of the process, of the merry chase. As my great-grandmother's poem says, "Tis well indeed she [success] knows." She knows that in the moment we turn around and face her, she's ready and waiting like Oprah, shouting, "You get a car! You get a car! You get a car!"

If you were to have a conversation with success, she would tell you, in essence, that Mr. Spock is right about having versus wanting. She would also add, "But don't let that stop you! After all, you've come this far."

"Lured By Her Witching Smile"

"You have to come to your closed doors before you get to your open doors... what if you knew you had to go through 32 closed doors before you got to your open door? Well, then you'd come to closed door number eight and you'd think, 'Great, I got another one out of the way'... Keep moving forward." – Joel Osteen

My great-grandmother's poem observes that people who chase success may do so for weeks, months and years:

"For we have followed her for so long. Lured by her witching smile."

Why do we do that?

In a word: Hope. Hope for a better tomorrow. Hope for a higher-paying job. Hope for more time with our family – although during the pandemic and lockdowns, many people have gotten that...or, if you have high-risk family members, perhaps not. But we have hope that life will improve. Gratitude helps, and a spirit of optimism. As we all know, it's easy to get discouraged when you don't see your life improving, but that witching smile of success keeps us going forward toward positivity.

I love Joel Osteen's uplifting message about welcoming the closed doors in your search to find the open one – the right door for us. He never sugarcoats the difficulties we face in life – he just encourages us to avoid becoming embittered or cynical in our pursuit of success for ourselves, our families, and friends, and dare I say it, our success as World Game-Changers. Because success can come at a price...

"All The Things/We Now Find Most Worthwhile"

"I look within to find my treasures." – Louise Hay

Have you ever had this experience? You are awake in the early morning hours, unable to turn your mind off. You start a running list of worries in your mind:

- ❖ "I've gotten what I want, so why am I anxious?"
- ❖ "What I want is within reach, so why am I thinking about all the ways tomorrow could go wrong?"
- ❖ "I really wanted this project/job/opportunity/relationship, so why am I thinking about how much stress I'll be under now? And how much less free time/quiet time with friends and family I'll have?"

Ungrateful? Maybe. But in chasing success, hoping for a different life, visualizing it and creating affirmations, we are willing to give up our former reality. We are willing to make a change.

As my great-grandmother's poem says: "We left behind us all the things/We now find most worthwhile." Sometimes that can be good – especially if those things are our excuses. excuse might be, "I don't have the time," "I'm too young," "I'm too old," "I don't have the right connections,""It's a bad time in the world,""No matter how hard I try, I can't fix my relationships," and so on.

Whenever I've looked my excuses in the face (with the help of family, friends and mentors who say, "You know you're just making excuses, right?"), they disappear, and the uncertainty sets in, especially at three a.m.

But if I truly get quiet and move past the anxiety, I hear the love and support and guidance of my friends and family. And I feel grateful. As Louise Hay wrote, I discover my treasures within.

"Till We Are Tired And Old"

The final stanza of my great-grandmother's poem might sound less than optimistic, but I can read it one of two ways. One, it's a lament. Two, it's more of a gentle question asking us to think about success and what we really want.

> "Success, you jade elusive sly,
> Must you always withhold
> The treasures at the rainbow's end
> 'Till we are tired and old?"

Chasing after success is normal. We seem to be hard-wired for it. But to return to the point made by Matthew McConaughey at the beginning of this chapter, it's how we define success that becomes the game-changer. It's the difference between jeopardizing your soul and discovering the treasures within as well as at the rainbow's end.

KristinJohnson.net

127

Frank Clark (UK)
Lucky Jim And His Guitar

I was born and bred in County Durham – around 8 miles from Newcastle – in the north-east of England. My father was a hard-working coal miner and as an only child, I fondly remember my early years. My over-riding recollection was of enjoying a warm, loving and secure upbringing; although I don't think I was ever told by either of my parents how much they loved me – but their actions certainly reinforced that I was.

As was the way in those days in our industrial communities, families were very tight-knit and mine was no different. Once again, I recall my extended family showing lots of love and support to me, within a sports-oriented background; my dad was a good golfer.

As I reflect back upon my life – and how lucky I've been – I often think about the timeless 'nature v nurture' debate; such as how a naturally gifted Northern Irish football player like George Best for example, would have turned out if he hadn't been nurtured and heavily influenced by the football-crazy Belfast communities.

I suppose the message is, talent alone is not enough – it needs to be supplemented with a strong work ethic and a healthy mind-set. I was grateful for nature being kind and giving me a height of 6-foot 1 inch – combined with 12-stones 2 pounds of weight.

Having enjoyed the immense benefits of being raised in a secure and loving family, my first awareness of pain – both physical and emotional – came when I was 20. I was playing for Crook Town Football Club at the time and had every intention of going onto university, after completing my A-levels.

However, fate had other plans for me; my A-level results were not good enough to get me a place at university and this disappointment lingered with me for a while; causing me some short-term emotional discomfort – I wasn't used to things not turning out as I has planned; a big lesson learnt for me – that's life, deal with it!

128

I subsequently signed as a professional footballer for Newcastle United Football Club (NUFC) and my prior emotional challenge was soon to be followed by a more physical one – I broke my leg. Treatment in those days was very sparse – there's only so much you can do with a bucket of cold water and a sponge – and so I was out of action for 11 months.

The big question at the back of my mind was 'Can I bounce back from this?' This temporary uncertainty was compounded further by the death of my dad. On the back of these major challenges – in a relatively short space of time – I consciously took the lessons from it all and moved on as best I could.

As a professional footballer, I was also having to distance myself from my old friends; my new-found focus as a professional athlete meant I had become far more aware of what was important to me and for me to continue to grow, I would need to leave some people and things from the past, behind.

This necessary detached approach was helped significantly by the fact that I spent some time in the NUFC reserve team – a very lonely place to be at times! With all due respect to most of the old pros that accompanied me in the reserves, they were not the most inspiring role models; they were at the end of their careers and I had barely even started mine.

Undeterred, I had the mindset to use this to my advantage; rather than dwell on my (temporary) misfortune, I used it as leverage to inspire and drive me on to bigger and better things – I would not become a victim of self-pity.

When I broke my leg, I was on the verge of breaking into the first team at NUFC. At the time, a player called George Dalton played the old-fashioned wing-half position; but the team manager – Joe Harvey – converted George to a left back, which was my key position too.

One month later, George got injured and I got my chance; I played the last two games of the 1963-64 season and from that point onwards, was never out of the team for the following 11 years; quite a contrast to today's squad rotation policy that seems to be favoured by a lot of modern-day managers.

To say life was prosperous would be an under-statement akin to the question 'Does the sun rise in the morning'! The Dolce Vita night club in Newcastle became my haven – life was truly blissful; compounded by winning the Fairs Cup with NUFC in June 1969, beating Hungarian side Ujpest Dozsa 6-2 over two games.

Shortly after, I met my wife – Pamela – when I was 27. Historically, football managers encourage young, single players to settle down with a wife and Joe Harvey was certainly no different; rationalising that the stability and responsibility of family life is far more conducive to players' careers than living the high life of a single man.

Interesting how – initially – there was role reversal here; I provided Pam with the stability she needed because she had a challenging time whilst growing up. However, such an 'investment' from me into a wonderful person like Pam would be paid back multi-fold in future years!

The 1974-75 season was my last at NUFC; there was a left-back – Alan Kennedy – that was starting to challenge for my number 3 shirt and I intuitively felt that this was probably the beginning of the end; increased further by an opportunity to go to America and become part of the ever-growing soccer revolution there.

Undeterred though – and not one to give in – I approached Joe and sought reassurances about my future. He set up a meeting with the chairman – Lord Westwood – with the latter categorically asserting 'You're going nowhere!' On the strength of this, Pam and I invested in a new house.

However, this assured security was to be extremely short-lived; in a matter of only weeks later, I was given a free transfer. Looking back, I suppose that was my first introduction to the cliché of 'there's no sentiment in football'. Once again, I found myself needing to change things; not helped by my missing out on the previous opportunity to go to America.

Within no time at all, I received an unflattering invitation to join the renowned manager Brian Clough at Nottingham Forest Football Club (NFFC); with his opening line to me being 'I'm desperate and need someone cheap – how you fixed?' This humble beginning was to become the start of a long association with NFFC as a player, manager, chairman and ambassador.

After spending 4 years as a player with Cloughie, I went to Sunderland AFC as assistant manager; I was there for 2 years before being sacked – paving the way for the manager's role at Leyton Orient Football Club (LOFC) for 9 years, before returning to NFFC as manager between 1993-1996.

The point of me highlighting these various moves, is the approach I adopted to embrace one of the certainties of life – uncertainty (change). My advice to anyone – regarding this aspect of life – is accept whatever's happening and get on with it.

Always maintain a positive mindset and actively look out for new opportunities – welcoming change is one of the secrets to success – be ready! I'm not saying it's easy, but it's certainly easier than allowing negative thoughts to take over and totally cloud and confuse the issue.

The way I see it, it's a question of focus and not becoming distracted by external conditions that you have no control over – ultimately, you are only responsible for your own actions.

This objective laser-like focus is – I humbly believe – a trait of successful people. Indeed, Hylton Smith (an author from my native north-east of England) once described me as 'one of the most organised and tactical people I've ever known'.

The awareness of my internal thinking to handle the change process was certainly put to the test with a more external event that presented itself in 1995; which was to change the landscape of European football dramatically – the Bosman Ruling – and more specifically, added further constraints to the role of being a foot-ball manager.

Within a month of leaving NFFC, I got the manager's job at Manchester City Football Club; but it was a huge relief when City sacked me. Through all the stresses and strains that go with foot-ball management, I survived because of my own self-belief and one other vital factor – my family.

Pam's influence in my life has been an immeasurable and very stabilising factor; whilst I was at LOFC, she was an absolute rock. She – and our two beautiful daughters – gave me reasons to keep strong, grounded and keep going; sometimes against all the odds.

Whilst I pride myself on never taking the job home with me, I'm sure there were times when Pam saw through things; but she just maintained her strength and supported me anyway. My wonderful family are undoubtedly part of a great legacy.

This legacy also includes – contributing towards making other people happy. Since retiring from football management at the age of 55 – I have come to realise the importance of everyday things like smiling at people and wishing them a good morning – it literally is the simple things in life that make a difference.

I believe I've always been a good delegator; empowering people to work towards a clearly-communicated vision that is supported by the right mind-set and values. As well as my own life legacy, I fervently believe I helped contribute towards strong positive legacies in football too – particularly at NUFC, LOFC and NFFC.

If I had to single out one person that has helped me create my football legacy, it would be a gentleman by the name of Bart Harwood; he was responsible for starting the under-11's school football team and igniting my passion for playing 'The Beautiful Game'.

The title of my story – Lucky Jim & His Guitar – reflects how fortunate I have been to have lived such a great life; with the guitar element embracing another very key passion in my life – music. When I was around 13 or 14, Lonnie Donegan burst onto the scene with his skiffle-style of music.

This form of entertainment has been a great source of happiness and comfort in my life – in good times and bad – and I particularly recall with fondness, my own rendition of 'Worried Man Blues'. I've sung this song all over the world; making my 'singing debut' at the 100 Club in London's Oxford Street in 1997.

It is my sincere wish that you have managed to take some

inspiration from my journey and I would like to close by offering two more insights:

> WOW: The best team always wins – the rest is only gossip
> (Jimmy Sirrel)

Janice Veech (USA)

Live From The Inside Out

I am experiencing a level of resistance unknown to me over writing this chapter. I have found myself struggling with this for days and now weeks. I feel much like a rudderless boat unable to maintain a direction. I ask myself why? Is it the title, subject matter, at this exact time in our timeline continuum that is so disconcerting? Why now? Why this?

These last weeks I have witnessed friends, family, and those of my friends line up to take an injection that makes absolutely no sense and exposes them to life-long consequences. So perhaps my faith and hope in Inner Truth and being able to convey my Inner Truth with kindness and clarity is shaken. I find myself reacting in astonishment and complete hopelessness that the people I love are joyfully exposing themselves to real and life-threatening risks. It breaks my heart. Sometimes I fall into thinking that it would be easier to be asleep and unaware. We are all being tested. And today at this time it seems that the opposite of awake, is denial.

I get that it is a Divine Unfolding, something as a collective we must go through. Because just on the other side of chaos emerges complexity and with complexity we evolve and ascend to the next dimension.

Almost exactly one year ago I saw Dr. Fauci for the very first time on TV. I could see a very dark entity in control of him. I saw this darkness oozing out of every visible orifice. It was pure evil intent, and it was in control. Moreover when I listened to what was spewing from this entity, my intuition and Higher Wisdom warned me that the message contained blatant lies. I was in shock.

What I couldn't understand though was why more people didn't see or at least intuit this. I learned quickly to discuss the rhetoric as falsehood. And I started to do my own research. I stopped watching mainstream media. I turned the TV off and instead looked to others questioning the rhetoric. The science being broadcast over the airways has never made sense to me. I come from a background of inquiry. I have a biology degree from Northwestern University where I also studied virology. I ran a Pulmonary Medical Research Lab at the University of Illinois Medical Center conducting ion transfer experiments across the mucous membrane of the trachea in hopes of unlocking the key to Cystic Fibrosis. I am a published in a medical journal. I went on and on like this. And then I sat in my own perspective channel and became reactive and argumentative with those who didn't see my perspective. And I stayed reactive and argumentative for longer than I care to acknowledge.

I fell into the mentality of "being right". Being right is deeply ingrained in the human psyche. We have programs operating in the background, our subconscious mind that train us to feel as if our very worth and identity is threatened if we are "wrong". By holding onto my need to be right, I received struggle in return. What I have found to be more beneficial is to ask yourself this question. Are you living from the outside in, or are you living from the inside out? Are you taking in mainstream media's version which promotes living in the hormones of stress and fear? Or are you listening to your Higher Wisdom, your Divine Authority as guidance? Consider the vibrational frequency opposites of these two states of being.

The question is not whether or not I was right. Perhaps a better question might be, "Is my perspective useful?" Or better yet does it make me happy? If not can I find a more positive and neutral perspective. So who is right and who is wrong? All of us. Each one of us, given our paradigm, points of view, and unique perspectives has our own truth. My truth is right for me as I'm sure your's is right for you.

There is a truth, and it guides us along a path of least resistance to love. All souls must decide for themselves. I realized I was coming from a place of judgement. I strive to allow others to have their own truths. It gets very, very difficult when my truths are polar opposites, 180 degrees different from those of my children, family members, and friends. I struggle with this.

My need to be "right" comes from a fear that those I care about can't find their way. Why is it so important to be "right" for anyone else but myself? We all have our roles to play in creation. But as a mother of three boys, now men, I struggle. So I return to my yoga mat every morning to find my way. I do Kundalini Yoga, Meditation, and IHS SACRED every day to strengthen my life force, my vital energy, my light. It is my most precious resource. I connect with the Divine daily. I merge with my Higher Wisdom to discern what is my truth and my role in the Ascension for the new paradigm. I know that the work that I do elevates my frequency to the highest possible consciousness frequency. And in turn my work elevates the frequency of everyone with whom I am connected.

I strive to live from the Inside Out, not the Outside In. From going deep within, I know that society is conditioned to believe vaccines prevent diseases. They don't. What they do is introduce diseases. Nanochips programmed to track and control individuals, as well as foreign tissue that can change your body's DNA are claimed to be vaccines. They are not. The good news is that these injections cannot keep you from Source. What does affect the journey is the energy of thoughts, feelings, and intentions. When those are fear, greed, betrayal, brutality, dishonesty, trauma, lack, and separation programming or any other low-frequency vibration or action, the energy generated decreases light within the body. Light is your body's life force. As we ascend we become more light and less matter.

Light keeps intensifying around the planet. And cells of people who are absorbing light are becoming crystalline. Light is what transforms carbon-based cells into the crystalline structure which strengthens immune systems and enables vitality and radiance in the higher vibrations of 4D & 5D. Earth is already vibrating in 5D and it is where we as a collective are striving to ascend. This is where intention and manifestation are simultaneous. It is simply a unification of desire with the outcome of that desire as a simultaneous manifestation rather than a linear process between desire and outcome.

I facilitate what I have coined Weaving Sessions every Friday, starting last October. I weave three different modalities that I have extensively studied and taught. We do Kundalini Yoga to elevate our frequencies to work with our Ka bodies. We separate our Ka body from our physical bodies, and we literally step into a new body template which allows us to work in the 5th Dimension to co-create the world in which we choose to live.

We are assisted and guided by Avatars, Benevolent Galactics, Arch Angels, Selfic Beings and Ascension guides. We are a growing band of light warriors. It is what gives me the most hope because we are making a difference in the world. We gather in person in Boulder, CO or via Zoom every Friday 4:00-5:30 pm MT. If this resonates with you and you want to actively co-create with us, we would love to have you join. Please contact me and I will send you the zoom link.

The transmutation from carbon to crystalline results in activated cellular memory. It opens Divine Remembrance of all past lives, bringing awareness and accessibility to all of the gifts and skills that you have honed over lifetimes. When you hold this cellular memory in its activated state, you hold your Divine Wisdom. You act from your inner Divine Authority. This is perceived by you as "knowing" or clairsentience and also as wisdom. Knowledge is activated, DNA is restructured to divine blueprint grids, and stargate ascension takes place. You will hold wisdom. The bliss of life is thus experienced once this state is achieved. You will be radiant. This is service to others and then just your energetic presence will elevate others. Once we begin to radiate en-masse then our entire planetary timeline and dimension shifts into the like-vibrations of that which you create.

As we integrate the ever-increasing vibrational frequencies bathing our Earth at this time, we experience changes in our physical, emotional, and etheric bodies. And we step into this new body template where intention and manifestation are simultaneous. We are to seek harmonious, higher frequency vibrations of light in all things. Knowledge alone can have the capacity to divide. But by applying Knowledge actively via Weaving Sessions we are able to go deeply within and gain a felt sense in the body of our truths. This is where soul awareness and wisdom unite. We experience Unity and are masters of our energy fields.

I listened to the 14th Pauri of Guru Nanak's Japji Sahib this morning. Japji is a Mantra for Kundalini Awakening. The 14th Pauri is a Mantra for Finding the Path. The English transliteration is as follows:

As I surrender to the path, as I align my will with the will of the Creator, Doubt drops away and my faith, in my self and my reality, grows with each day.

When you agree, Your path becomes clear. When you agree, you go Home shining with honor.

When you agree, You are not of this world. When you agree, You embrace the Dharma.

Such is the Nam. It makes you pure. If you agree to agree, Your mind becomes pure.

The key to your freedom is the Love and Light you carry inside of you.

There are many "truths". Go within. Find your deeper truths and live according to them.

Connect with your Higher Wisdom and your Divine Authority and let the Divine guide you.

Live From The Inside Out…

Paul Hart (UK)

Giving Youth A Sporting Chance

I made my name in professional football as a centre-half, making my debut in 1970 for Stockport County; my playing career spanned 18 years – amassing 567 appearances and scoring 49 goals in the process. I began my management career at Chesterfield Football Club in 1988.

I was born in a place called Golborne – a mining village near Haydock Park Racecourse, England – and lived in a council house. My Dad Johnny Hart, used to travel to Manchester City Football Club's Maine Road ground, until he stopped playing in 1960; he was an inside-forward for City and then became their manager.

Only then – after Dad purchased a house from the football club, did I really start to become aware of football; whilst also realising what a popular figure he was at Manchester City.

Although my brother Nigel – 5 years my junior – and I were both reared in a loving, stable family environment, we rarely got to see Dad in our earlier years. Mum finished work in 1953 once I was born and although times were times were hard – rationing was still around – we always had a full larder; as a family, we particularly understood the value of food.

From the age of around 7-8, I slowly began to fall in love with football. Throughout the 1960's I began to progress through schools' football and I vividly recall how Dad used to try everything he could, to deter me from pursuing a career as a professional; he didn't think I was good enough. At 17, I got my first professional contract at Stockport County.

Dad regularly tore into me as a schoolboy; although I'm sure this chastisement was based upon some kind of management psychology and certainly for my own good. Once I'd signed professional forms however, he was totally unswerving in his support for me.

As I enter my 47th year in football – despite any inadequacies – I feel I've had a decent career and certainly one that has provided me with a prosperous life.

In terms of pain, this – like everything else in my life – is all in the context of football.

As a centre-half where, the obligatory 'designer nose' was earned the hard way – along with my broken leg – physical pain is something that comes and goes. At the age of 35, I had to deal with a different kind of pain – finishing my playing career!

I'd already done my A-licence coaching badge and in 1987, I was invited to go to Notts County as a player/ coach. Following a year of cutting my 'coaching teeth' I then went to nearby Chesterfield Football Club as a manager.

After getting the sack there, I went to Leeds United as Academy Director – employed by Howard Wilkinson – and it was there that I found my passion for youth football.

I realised I wanted to work with kids and used all the good principles I'd learned as a player. I'd worked under some really good managers, including a certain Brian Clough and I was determined to pass these positive traits – such as using good manners, having respect for referees and not feigning injury etc – onto the young players under my charge.

As a leader, I knew what I stood for and what I stood against and things were not up for compromise! Within my management positions, it was up to me to set the standard and ensure we all followed through on those things; as Cloughie often used to say 'From the Chairman to the tea-lady'. I believe creating a clear, positive culture is critical in any organisation if success is to be achieved.

Paul Lowe recently reminded me of something I'd said to him in 2000 – when I was the Academy Director at Nottingham Forest – whilst Paul was working as part of the team delivering the education programme to the young apprentice footballers.

At the end of the season, certain players would be released and Paul said to me 'It's that heart-breaking time of the year again gaffer'. My candid response being 'Always remember, they'll leave this club as even better young men than they were, when they first came here'.

The thing is, these young men knew – that despite having to break the news that some wouldn't be kept on as a professional – we really cared about them. As mentors, we had a moral duty to make sure these boys felt valued and respected; you need to know you matter and someone cares about you and in my opinion, this is a fact of life – not just in the world of football.

For me, it was about making positive changes – bit by bit – and continually practising those new lessons learnt, so they became embedded within their lives and became a way of being. It's the little things that matter in life and I know by paying attention to the details, that a bigger – far more beneficial – picture emerges.

In 1978, I was Leeds United Football Club's record signing and I remember going through a very challenging phase of my life; I can only liken it to being in a dark tunnel – probably due to the power of expectation and the fact that I wasn't playing very well.

It's amazing at times like this, how much your self-belief gets tested and I instinctively knew in my own mind, I had to work through this stark period and emerge from it victorious. I don't know if I would describe it as depression, but I felt unhappy and it was certainly a scary place to be at times.

A low phase raised its head again once my playing career had finished; being stripped of your sense of purpose, focus and routine – not to mention significance in life – can be an extremely challenging ordeal to cope with. To compound this pain, I never really had a great sense of self-awareness then.

This was epitomised by the fact that I never perceived myself to be a good player; I responded more to being given simple instructions. These days though, I now realise the critical importance of self-awareness; I believe it to be the solid foundation from which everything else in life will progress and grow.

It's futile to have regrets – you cannot change the past, only learn lessons from it – but one of the things I sometimes think about, is I wish I'd been more sensitive towards other people. I'm noticing these days, that I'm becoming more resistant to change.

Forgiveness is something that I generally struggled with – it takes a long time for me to do so with people; although I'm very aware I've had more than my fair share of forgiveness from others.

Interesting – particularly in the world of football – how you learn to develop a different façade; mine was one of being a stern-face, resolute character. The contradiction of this is the many young people that I have been involved in managing within football have seen my 'real' softer side.

Having achieved many successful goals in my life – not just in football – I reflect on what it will have all counted for; in other words, what would be my legacy? Ultimately, I'd like to think others thoughts towards me are 'He's a good bloke'. That said, I firmly believe it's more important to have self-validation, rather than rely on external feedback.

Part of my own moral compass, is to constantly teach good values to others and lead through example – by committing to my own top 5 values of honesty, respect, humility, learning and development. My vision is simple: to inspire and influence people to become the very best they can be.

> WOW: Always strive to create your own legacy
> – be kind and caring

Sally Hooper (USA)

Choose Hope

Faith and fear both demand you to believe in something you can't see. You choose.
(Bob Proctor)

When a loved one has a condition that is elusive in terms of a cure, you begin searching and shopping – for solutions and cures.

It often takes more than just time to find them. Sometimes they remain evasive, zapping you of both time and energy that may already be in short supply. For me, it becomes essential to simultaneously look for hope. You will no doubt find it if you open your heart to receiving it, as hope is never in short supply.

Along each journey to find whatever it was that I was looking for, my holy grail, I have always been blessed to find hope. Sometimes that hope came by way of connecting with someone who was on the other side of a similar mountain and prevailed. Other times it arrived as if by divine intervention… an article in a magazine I picked up, or a news story that lifted a corner of the veil I was after. Occasionally it was necessary to conjure it up, out of thin air, just to balance out the darkness.

Hope can shine an exquisite light on a path forward, and fuel you to continue on, leaving no stone unturned… because something monumentally important to you depends on it. When you are out on the edge, staring into the abyss of darkness, it is helpful to believe in something. Anything really. Often faith and hope are the only things that will carry you through. They have for me at least.

Hope… It's what you have when you have nothing
else. And if you have it, you have everything.

Despite being fairly well-rounded at many things medical, food allergy was not on my radar. Not in the least bit. So when my son

Zayne was about fifteen months old, I thought nothing of giving him a piece of toast with peanut butter. He was expanding his food repertoire at a slow trot and I was hopeful peanut butter toast could be added to his short little list of options. It was a little strip of toast with only a smear of peanut butter. I didn't want him to choke. He didn't. He reacted

It was odd, that red rash on his face around his mouth. It looked like red dye had spilled on him and was wiped off leaving a bright stain. Zayne was still in his high chair and only a few nibbles in. I quickly took the toast from him and washed his face… as if I could simply wipe away a food allergy with a diaper wipe.

The next morning I gave Zayne another smear of peanut butter, but on a graham-cracker. Within seconds the mysterious red rash materialized again out of nowhere. Poof! Bingo… he was allergic to peanut butter! Now, was it the peanuts, the palm oil, or the molasses in the peanut butter? Only kidding. I didn't subject him to that. What I did do was avoid peanut butter until his next pediatrician appointment. What I didn't do was panic. I didn't know enough to panic. I didn't understand anaphylaxis yet. Turns out I wouldn't for some time. After all, it was 2002 and my phone wasn't smart. I also knew nobody with a food allergic child, and I knew nobody who knew anybody with a food allergic child either.

Our pediatrician seemed unimpressed, "It sounds like he's allergic to peanuts, so just avoid them." That was it… literally. There was no come to Jesus about epinephrine, Benadryl, or cross-contamination. And ignorance was bliss. And so, we carried on avoiding them, or trying.

Without asking permission, time carried on. And while it ticked, I soaked up every bit of cuddly goodness being Zayne's mommy. He was nearly two and a half by the time we finally landed at an allergist's office for a reality check. With a few more allergic incidents having occurred and a new diagnosis of asthma, it was time. At our first appointment, I casually mentioned the nut allergy. The doctor asked if I needed a prescription refill on my EpiPen. An epi-what?

There it was, initiation into the Food Allergy Mom Club. It was overdue. Along with the initiation, I received the bad and the ugly on anaphylaxis and cross-contamination. There was no good. Until then allergy had equaled rash, hives, sneezing and itching. Shortness of breath, low blood pressure and a swollen airway were something else entirely. Today I shudder at the gravity of risk we were taking, moving through life clueless and EpiPen-less, not yet knowing he was also allergic to every single other nut, and peas and sesame too.

With enough understanding of the life-threatening nature of food allergies to scare the bejesus out of me, I pledged to advance my allergy acumen. I ordered books and read them all. I researched treatments and found out there weren't any. I learned that only 18% percent of kids will outgrow a nut allergy and that percentage goes down with each accidental exposure. The more I learned, the more I panicked. Every time Zayne opened his mouth to eat, I felt the paralyzing grip of fear

Hope is being able to see that there is light despite all of the darkness. (Desmond Tutu)

Fear is a powerful motivator though, and it moved me to create a reality I could tolerate, and he could survive in. I worked overtime, establishing logistics that could accomplish both. I educated anyone who would listen and insisted others listen too. I encouraged everyone in his orbit to avoid nuts and required hand washing before interacting with him. I began calling manufacturers and interrogating their quality control people about ingredients and cross-contamination, as warnings on labels weren't a thing yet. I ensured that his life saving medicine was always within reach. I even carried two EpiPens with different lot numbers in case one was faulty or in the event of a bi-phasic reaction requiring a second dose. And still, I wondered if I had missed something.

I also looked for the light, as living with the burden of food allergies was heavy, and I could not reconcile it being his life sentence. With what I had left in the tank, I kept one eye on the latest research, as I desperately needed to believe there would be a cure in his life-time. I had faith in science, and that faith gave me hope.

Soon it was time for Zayne to start pre-school. By then he had a baby sister, Elle. She grew up nut-free too. That way they could snuggle and double-dip without paramedics involved. For most families, starting pre-school is an exciting milestone. For us, it was terrifying. I tried to convince myself he would develop normally if I just kept him in a bubble instead. Unconvinced, I looked for a pre-school where I could breathe after saying goodbye at drop-off. I interviewed directors and most importantly, observed during snack and lunchtime.

Eventually I found one, and I never regretted the decision to deflate the bubble idea. Zayne was their first student with life-threatening food allergies (as he would be in every grade moving forward). So I blazed a trail where there had been no path. With permission, I trained the staff on food allergies and anaphy-laxis, complete with expired EpiPens and oranges to jab them in. I spent hours preparing for it all, as my child's life literally depended on it. The pre-school director then invited me to train the parents too, who were incredibly understanding and compassionate.

Zayne made amazing friends in pre-school. I'm sure it helped that he was a well-mannered and kind-hearted child, but the loyalty these families showered on my son was unexpected. While I was busy teaching Zayne how to shimmy into a lunch bench keeping his hands sterile, these parents were teaching their boys compassion and empathy. They loyally sat with my son each and every day with packed lunches safe enough for even Zayne. And if Zayne said "no thank you" to a special treat offered, so did they. I worried someone would come along and pinch me. Thankfully, nobody did.

Meanwhile, I taught Zayne a level of self-restraint that most grownups don't possess. No shared food or drinks ever, regardless of how hungry or thirsty you are! No food or drinks unless they are parent sanctioned, despite how decadent and delicious they may look, and even if another grown up tells you it's safe. It was indoctrination. It was brainwashing. It was life-saving. Zayne was bright and always seemed to understand the seriousness of it all. The psycho-social burden carried by a food allergic family can't be denied. Food allergies make you chronically vulnerable and the overarching and far-reaching hypervigilance required, makes it all simply exhausting to navigate. As such, I also indoctrinated him with hope… "Don't worry my sweet, we're going to find a cure, this won't be forever." I needed to chant that mantra perhaps more than he needed to hear it. It fueled me to deliver on that promise and to keep him alive in the interim.

We slipped into quite a groove with all our precautions and protocols in place. I set cruise control and kept us all in the nut-free lane. We largely avoided accidental exposures, except for that one birthday party where a fellow four-year-old attendee had eaten cashews and mistakenly used Zayne's snorkel before Zayne used it again unknowingly. Yes, the reaction required an EpiPen and his 18% chance of outgrowing it all, slipped a little further away. Still, I maintained hope. I just knew that this could not be our reality forever and I reminded him of that too.

Every couple years my precious boy would have blood work done to see if he were any less allergic. Zayne couldn't help but get his hopes up, just as I secretly did. It was demoralizing for him to get his results back only to find out his levels were worse than before. He wasn't in that coveted 18% and we both knew it. Still, I'd lean-in and whisper, "Don't worry my sweet, we'll find a cure." I said that on repeat every time his morale dipped, even adding "I promise."

Years passed and my boy with a golden heart and an old soul became a teenager. It snuck up on me. I kept up with the research on a type of treatment called oral immunotherapy (OIT). While in its infancy, it was promising. By the time Zayne was fourteen and had taken to training his friends how to use an EpiPen, I read about a doctor who was doing a unique version of OIT with precision medicine, individualized protocols, and astounding results. Dr. Randhawa was able to achieve food freedom for his patients.

I almost dismissed him as a charlatan, preying on the hopeless by peddling hope. But then, as if by divine intervention, I received validation.

Having recently moved, we found the kids a new pediatrician. At the first appointment with her, I brought up Zayne's life-threatening food allergies. The doctor interjected, "Oh, the physician I bought this practice from had two grandchildren allergic to nuts and they are fine now, eating nuts and everything."

I proceeded to interrogate her on the subject and it turned out those kiddos were treated by Dr. Randhawa, the very same doctor I had nearly dismissed as too good to be true. It was a fortunate stroke of serendipity really... me randomly picking out the pediatrician who lifted a corner of the veil.

Our hope balloon was inflating. It took me a few weeks to track this mysterious doctor down. His phone line connected to voicemail with a cryptic outgoing message. Nevertheless, I left one myself. Eventually I heard back and learned there was a waitlist – a long one averaging three years. I immediately put Zayne on it and continued my vetting while we waited. I also signed up to hear Dr. Randhawa speak.

A few weeks later, my husband and I joined a few hundred other desperate parents in an auditorium bubbling over with both hope and skepticism... but mostly hope. It was clear pretty quickly that the doctor had revolutionized oral immunotherapy. He declared a simply stated goal... food freedom for all food allergic children. I tried to reconcile the apparent simplicity of that statement with the ambition it would take to achieve it. He spoke of individualized treatment plans based on each patient's immune response to determine a course of treatment for their specific system. I wanted one for Zayne.

He spoke of his safety record, near-perfect success rate, how no case was too complicated and no allergy too severe. I wanted to believe him. He spoke of his outcome data and eating without restriction after treatment. I imagined that life for my son. He reminded us that 15–20 million people suffer potential anaphylaxis each and every day, yet only a few thousand nationally are currently receiving some form of OIT.

I did the math. He explained how a decade of diagnostic data had yielded 180 million data points, and when combined with high power mathematics and analytics, precision treatment resulted. My holy grail wore a white lab coat.

Dr. Randhawa spilled hope into the hall and into parents who had all but lost theirs. Parents whose only remaining hope came in an auto-injector at an extortion price and with an expiration date. I let that hope seep in, and it did more than that. It seeped in and even began to soak up some of the fear I had grown accustomed to. Without saying a word, my husband and I looked at each other with wide eyes and a smile. The subtitles read, "I think we found his cure!"

Those who wish to sing, always find a song.
(Swedish Proverb)

We had wished to sing, and we found the most perfect song!

Eventually Zayne worked his way off what ended up being "only" a two-year waitlist. It was his turn. After two years of intense treatment, Zayne arrived at food freedom. Today he can eat however much he wants, whenever he wants, of anything he wants. Peanuts are his favorite.

I had spent enough time over the years imagining Zayne dying from anaphylaxis. Each iteration was as horrible as the next. There is one where he's found slumped over in a bathroom stall, too shy to have asked for a buddy to go with him to the restroom when his stomach hurt. In another, he and his girlfriend make out, forgetting she ate an off-limits granola bar. I lose my son and she loses her mind. I had even imagined a wheelchair bound, drooling, non-verbal Zayne in a diaper. He survived anaphylaxis only to be left brain damaged from going without oxygen for too long. But with Zayne's food freedom, came freedom from this fear. The fear had served its purpose though, so I thanked it with gratitude and then let it go.

Food allergy parents are champions for their children, and hopeful ones at that. We relentlessly pursue improved outcomes, compassionate friends, and affordable epinephrine. We explain, re-explain, train, and retrain. We have uncomfortable conversations with our teenager's boyfriends and girlfriends. We board planes early with bleach wipes and educate the flight crew. We bake safe treats, host all parties, volunteer for every soccer snack, and ask to speak with either the manager or the chef at every restaurant.

We call ahead, call again, and call somewhere else when necessary. We do this in hope of creating a safer environment for our children. We created our own training for schools before prefab ones existed. Before the Food Allergen Labeling and Consumer Protection Act became law in 2005, we spent hours on the phone each week with food manufacturers and quality control to find out about allergens, cross-contamination, and facility risks. We indoctrinate our kids with mantras like... no label-no thank you, don't risk it for the biscuit, and every label, every time. We explain how "sharing isn't always caring." We willingly host all sleepovers and interrogate science camp medics. We teach our children to advocate for themselves before it is developmentally appropriate. We donate pallets of wipes to schools to mitigate risk and bribe custodians to clean our child's classroom extra well. We make generous donations to classrooms to offset the responsibility of being our child's teacher. We avoid nuts ourselves so that we can freely kiss our littles. We insist on a nut-free table. Then we insist the school lunches be nut-free too, so any child with a hot lunch is welcome to sit at the nut-fee table and our child is less likely to eat alone. We reward the four loyal friends with goodies to reinforce that loyalty and compassion. We make sure the freezer in the school office is stocked with safe cupcakes in case there is a birthday that is not on our radar. We read, research, and raise awareness. We give extra candy to the little pirate who on Halloween says, "Trick-or-treat, I'm allergic to nuts." We tell them everything is safe and that our child is allergic too and then we wink at the pirate's mommy and say to ourselves "Bless you dear woman, I understand your path because

I walk it." We pack six Epi-pens and a few more expired ones when we fly. Then we dare someone in security to have an issue with it. We are fierce and resilient and hopeful. Hopeful.

What started as a tiny mustard seed of hope, kept me going all those years ago. Hope had me promising a cure to my son because I believed it to be true. And I simply allowed my faith in that mustard seed to be bigger than all my fear combined.

Jeannette Linfoot (UK)

If I Can Do It, So Can You!

The Early Years

I truly believe that each and every person has greatness within them, and we can achieve anything we want in life, however it's not always easy. The most powerful thing to have in your life is BELIEF – it all starts with the inner you. When you genuinely believe in yourself, you are clear on what you want in life and you're prepared to put the work in, then there are no limits; you can truly achieve anything you want.

It's not always easy to get to that place, and it certainly hasn't been for me, so I'm here to share my story with you, to help you and hopefully show that if I can do it, then so can you!

My story isn't a rags to riches story, nor is it one about bouncing back from trauma or tragedy, but it is one of internal struggle which I think will resonate with a lot of people.

When I look back at my life there has been this constant battle between imposter syndrome vs self-belief. I think this is the case for many people, and so much of this goes back to either things that have happened in the past that we've carried around for years or the stories that either ourselves or other people have told us over the years. These limiting self-beliefs can really hold us back, and this is something that I've had to work hard on myself to overcome. Even to this day, although thankfully less and less frequently now, the old imposter syndrome and voice in my head can kick in at times telling me 'I'm not good enough', 'I don't fit in' or 'I'm going to get found out'.

Here I am in my 40s as a £multi-million business owner, with financial freedom, flexibility and choice, an incredible partner, Chris, who I adore and wonderful family and friends who I am eternally grateful for. I genuinely do not say any of this to brag, as it wasn't always like that.

I grew up in Stretford in Manchester, the youngest of three daughters. I was 'the baby' of the family, a title which I rather quite

152

enjoyed. I was incredibly lucky and had a really happy childhood. We were a working-class family where both my parents, Doreen and Arthur, were both 'grafters', and those values of working hard were definitely instilled in me from an early age.

There was always a lot of love in the family and whilst we didn't want for anything – in fact were really lucky as mum and dad made sure we had family holidays abroad every year which they saved up hard to give us – we didn't have an abundance of money.

We were a 'normal' working-class family. Those core values of respect, honesty, hard work and treating people as you would like to be treated yourself are values that have stayed with me through my whole life.

Being the 'baby' of the family and the youngest of three daughters definitely had two sides to it for me. On the one hand, I loved being the youngest and I certainly got an easier ride than my elder sisters. However, the flip-side of it was that despite my parents always showing me lots of love, I was always looking for approval and reassurance that even though I was third in line, that at times I could be number one.

I can still see that little girl dancing in front of the stage, doing daft things to get attention, being a diligent student, otherwise known as a 'girlie swot', or whatever it was, but always looking for the approval and adoration. It was much later in life before I realised that this need to be loved and approved of – combined with the imposter syndrome – was a key theme in my life. Even to this day there are times when those old memories will surface, and I find myself seeking attention and positive affirmations that remind me I am good enough.

The norm for a family like ours was to follow a typical route of school, education, get a job, work hard, settle down, have a family, retire etc. However, I did have a role model in my mum who was quite entrepreneurial having had numerous jobs as a secretary but having a side-hustle as a market trader and then becoming her own boss opening a hardware store. I have fond memories of being about 7 years old working on the market with my mum and in the shop on a Saturday. Mum had a rebellious streak deep down, often much to the chagrin of my dad, even going off buying a caravan and a holiday cottage in North Wales without even telling him! Despite this and with dad being surrounded by women, he often fondly referred to us as the 'knicker brigade' and I loved being part of that gang!

Both my sisters, Alison and Andrea, got married young, had families and stayed local, which was great for them and I'm grateful for the wonderful families they created whom I feel very close to. However, as I got into my teenage years, I had a feeling that there was more to life than settling down in Manchester and having a family. I had no idea what I wanted to do, but I did know there was a big wide world out there and I wanted to be part of it. At a relatively early age I remember feeling a bit like the black sheep of the family.

The Black Sheep Breaking Out

Whilst I was very proud of where I was from and my work-ing-class routes, I couldn't wait to get out into the big wide world. That first step came with the chance to go to university. As the girlie swot I was, I had done well in my A-Levels, so off I went to Leeds University to study Economics. I was the only one to go to university in the family and it wasn't easy for my parents to be able to support me financially. They were very proud of me and never put pressure on me, but I certainly put the pressure on myself and felt the weight of responsibility to do well. Yet again those two behaviours of imposter syndrome and seeking approval would kick in on a regular basis.

I certainly burnt the candle at both ends, had an amazing time, made friends for life and came out with a first-class honours degree in Economics & Management Studies, which I was incredibly proud of.

I graduated in 1993, when there was a recession on and despite having a great degree and strong track-record, I was applying for literally hundreds of jobs and getting rejection after rejection. I was getting a bit desperate, and remember applying for the graduate scheme at McCaines, the chip makers, and even Rugby cement – oh the shame when I didn't even get accepted for those! Thank god I didn't, how different my life could have been – sometimes things happen for a reason.

The strong work ethic kicked in again and during that time I did anything to bring money in. I didn't want to have to ask mum and dad as they had already sacrificed so much for me to go to university. I had four jobs at the same time and must have been the most highly-qualified waitress at Old Trafford Cricket Club, post-delivery girl at Kelloggs, wiper of tables at Debenhams and waitress in the local restaurant.

Eventually through persistence, I got offered a job as a Government Economist down in Whitehall. I didn't really want to go to London, so I did the classic and said 'I'll go for 2-3 years max' – here we are 25 years later!

With that move to London, this again pushed me out of my comfort zone. I didn't know one single person, so it was quite a big deal at the time. When I got into the role, the imposter syndrome would rear its head again, as 70% of the people in the Government Economic Service were either Oxford or Cambridge graduates, and I'd got my degree from Leeds! Time and again I had to tell myself that my degree was as good as theirs and I did deserve to be there, but inside I didn't really believe it.

After a few years I realised that the grey cardigans of the civil service weren't for me, so I jumped into the travel industry where I then spent the rest of my corporate career for the next 25 years. To do so I actually took a step back and joined on the graduate scheme at Thomson, a UK travel company. Given that I had been working for two years already, to go back to the bottom and start again could have been judged as a crazy thing to do, but I knew that if I wanted to make a change then sometimes you need to take a backward step in order to move forwards. It was probably also linked to the fact that I'd applied to join Thomson when I was at university and got rejected, so perhaps it was the stubborn side of my personality to just persevere regardless of the rejection.

From there I had a great career in the travel industry working for some of the best brands in travel including Thomson, First Choice, Thomas Cook, TUI and Saga. I got promoted quickly and feel fortunate to have done some amazing roles. Essentially I started at the bottom and just kept going until I made it to becoming the MD of the Emerging Markets for TUI and the CEO of the Travel Division for Saga PLC. During those roles there were so many bumps in the road that I had to overcome and lots of things that didn't go right. This might sound familiar to you too, but what worked for me was being clear on where I wanted to get, which was ultimately to run a big business, telling my imposter syndrome gremlins to 'shut up' and consistently putting the work in, I got there in the end!

Leap Of Faith, Take A Deep Breath – How Bad Can It Be?

There's been a few pivotal moments in my career where I've had to take a leap of faith and despite the fear of failure, take a deep breath and give it a go! Clearly I had this when I made the move down to London and I had it again when I was asked by TUI to go to Barcelona to turn around three failing businesses. At the time I was 28 so relatively young for such a position, but I just thought give it a go, how bad can it be? If I mess it up at least I'll have learnt something and hopefully no-one's going to die in the process! Of course no-one died and I did a good job, which then spurred me on to the next challenge and opportunity.

The next big time when this happened to me was when I was Product Director for First Choice who had just merged with their competitor TUI. TUI had made a strategic decision to expand into the emerging markets, the first of which were Russia & Ukraine. I had been doing a big functional director role for a while so was ready for a change but had no idea what the next move would be.

I was then asked out of the blue if I fancied going to Russia to buy three businesses, rebrand them as TUI and launch to the market, I was a bit shocked. The imposter syndrome kicked in and I thought I can't do this, I have no idea how to do mergers and acquisitions, I've never done business in Russia, what if I fall flat on my face and so the gremlin voices went on and on. I'll be eternally grateful to my new boss at the time Richard Prosser, who saw something in me that I didn't see in myself. So off I went to Russia did high double digit £million acquisitions and launched TUI in Russia & Ukraine. Through that time every day I had doubts about whether I could do this, but I just kept going, brought on a great team around me and kept focused on the end goal. From there that led to me ultimately being promoted to MD of the Emerging Markets running an international business with interests across Russia, Ukraine, China, India, and South America. The big lesson here was trust in other people when they believe in you and if you put yourself in the way of opportunity, give it a go, keep the faith, and do the best you can, you never know where things can lead.

Kids Or No Kids Dilemma

As I got into my mid-30s and my career was really flying, I then had to decide whether I was going to have kids. Clearly this isn't a solo choice, and my partner Chris had a say too, but as a woman the perspective is different for sure. I always thought that I would have a family, but I also knew that I wanted to have a career. It certainly doesn't have to be the case of one or the other, and I'm full of admiration for women who have both, but for me I was ambitious on the career side and up to that point, hadn't put the same focus on having kids. Deep-down if I'm honest with myself, I think I was kicking the 'can down the road' and putting off making a decision until I really had to. I think this is something that a lot of women struggle with – the questions go round and round in your head, or at least they did in mine – do I really want kids? If I do then why haven't I done more to make it happen? Am I just thinking I should because that's what society expects? How will people judge me if I don't? If I don't have kids what kind of legacy do I leave? Does it make my presence on this earth less meaningful? On and on and on those questions went for a few years!

After much agonising, I realized that personally for me whatever I decided was my choice, and it really shouldn't matter what other people say or think on this, apart from Chris of course. Eventually after much wrangling, I came to a sense of peace with it all; but having made that decision not to have kids, I was still struggling to find what my legacy should be – 'if I haven't got kids then how do I leave a lasting mark on this world?' It took me a while to figure it out but when I did it felt like a huge burden and pressure had been lifted off my shoulders. I finally realised that I matter, I do count, and I can make my mark in a way that might be different to others but is equally important and impactful on this world.

The Only Woman In The Boardroom

Multiple times through my career I've often been the only woman in the boardroom with full profit & loss responsibility for the businesses I was leading. Navigating the alpha-male board room can be a pretty intimidating place, in particular for someone who can suffer with imposter syndrome like I have done at times. I remember when I got promoted to MD of the Emerging Markets for TUI and was reporting directly into Peter Long the Group CEO, I would think 'oh my god, what's a working-class girl from Stretford doing here?' and I would often have to remind myself that I was good enough to be there. Of course I was and in reality, Peter was incredibly supportive of me, so whilst the environment was very male-dominated, it was me who was self-sabotaging. It helped as I had a great ally in Jacky Simmonds, the HR Director, who set me up with an amazing mentor.

The tussle between imposter syndrome and self-belief were fighting it out good and proper, but thankfully self-belief won the fight! I always think that if you walk into a room thinking there will be a problem, then the chances are there will be, so you have to change the inner-dialogue. After all, generally what you look for, you will find, positive or negative.

I had to navigate similar waters when I moved to Saga as CEO of the Travel Division, which was a business that had been in decline and in desperate need of transforming and dragging kicking and screaming into the modern world of travel. In that role I was responsible for £340m of revenue, 1,700 people on my team and during the two years I was there I got the business back into double-digit growth at the same time as doubling the profit before tax from £8m to £15m, which I feel incredibly proud of. The business was incredibly traditional and although the Group CEO was more progressive in his thinking, there was definitely a lot of resistance to change, despite the positive results I was delivering. The big lesson for me at this time was to make sure I found the right environment where I could flourish, where my ambitions matched those of the organisation, and where I had wings to fly. If the fit isn't right, then have the confidence to move on.

I've loved my career in the corporate world and have no regrets, but when I decided to leave to become my own boss, which is where I am now with three of my own businesses and my podcast Brave, Bold, Brilliant, it was great to be in full control of my own destiny.

My Rock

The people you have in your life are critical. I'm lucky as I have a loving family, a mum who encourages and inspires me every day and great friends who I'm truly grateful for. My dear old dad Arthur passed away eight years ago, and I really miss him. There's not a day goes by that I don't think of him and I often ask myself 'what would dad say?'. Having positive people in your life, past and present, have made a huge difference to me being able to reach for the stars.

There is one special person who I feel so fortunate to have in my life and that's my amazing partner Chris, who is there by my side through thick and thin. Chris is in the unique position of being my biggest fan and my biggest critic all rolled into one. He will always encourage me to follow my dreams, push forward and backs me 100% with anything I want to do, often even if that involves him having to make sacrifices to help me get there. Equally there are plenty of times where he will 'call me out' if I'm off-track or maybe not tackling things in the best way. Sometimes it's a case of tough love, which can be hard to take, but it certainly keeps me on-track.

He often jokes that he's the Dennis to my Margaret Thatcher. Not sure I like being compared in every aspect to Maggie, but I'm sure you get the analogy, that behind successful people there's often a rock behind the scenes who plays a huge role in making that person successful. I'm eternally grateful to have Chris in my life.

Finding My True Purpose And Reason Why

From the journey I've been on and the lessons I've learnt along the way, I now feel that I've found my true purpose. On a personal basis it's all about leaving a strong financial and life legacy for my nieces and nephews, so that my immediate impact on those I love will carry on to the next generation and the one after that and so on.

It's not about having my own kids anymore. I adore my nieces and nephews and if I can think that they will look back with fondness and think 'auntie Net' was alright, then that makes me immensely happy – 'she was good fun, taught us a few things and set us up to be strong individuals, believing that we can achieve anything we want in life'

As far as having a wider impact on the world is concerned, I'm genuinely grateful for everything that I've had in my life and I truly believe that it would be a crime not to give back and to use the gifts I have for a wider good. My mission is to help as many people as possible unlock their true potential and live the life they dream of. Whether that's through mentoring, public speaking, my podcast, helping people as and when they need a friendly ear or a bit of support, or a combination of all of those.

Finally, I've found inner-peace that I am definitely good enough, I do belong, I am worth it, I am loved, I know exactly why I'm here and what is important to me.

If I Can Do it, So Can You

So as you can see I have had this constant tussle of imposter syndrome and seeking approval vs self-belief to power me forward. If you also have those feelings I hope my story has helped you in some small way.

I've learnt a lot along the way, made tons of mistakes, had ups, downs, been plagued with insecurities and doubt so I thought I'd end by sharing some pieces of advice that might help you, as they have helped me...

- ❖ Learn to love yourself. You are the only one that needs to be happy with who you are. You are unique and special in your own way and there is no one better at being you than you
- ❖ Believe in yourself and drop those limiting self-beliefs. You can achieve anything you want in life, but you have to truly believe in yourself
- ❖ Find your own true purpose. Your reason 'why' and journey will be different to mine and different to those around you, and that's fine, but make sure you live your dreams to the max
- ❖ Don't try to do what you think you should do to just please others, do what is right for you and your loved ones
- ❖ It's essential to have a clear destination you are heading but remember to enjoy the ride along the way too
- ❖ Strive to be the best version of yourself you can possibly be. We are all either growing or dying
- ❖ Be patient as the seeds you plant today will flower tomorrow, but you have to keep watering your garden for those seeds to flower
- ❖ Put your own oxygen mask on first. If you're not in good shape then you can't help those around you. Spend some part of everyday working on yourself. Every day I do my miracle morning, (1) spending some time in silence, (2) saying my affirmations out loud, (3) visualizing what I want to achieve, (4) reading so I learn something new, (5) writing meaningful notes down and (6) exercise. Find your own version of this but don't neglect self-care to keep your body and mind healthy
- ❖ Be grateful for what you have today in your life, otherwise you may never find true contentment
- ❖ Surround yourself with the right people, those who will support you, lift you up, call you out in a constructive way and

help you on your journey. Reduce the time you spend with those people who don't support you. Sometimes this might mean cutting people out of your life, which can be tough

❖ Ignore the naysayers, those who put you off or discourage you. They are not on your journey, you are, so it doesn't matter if they don't 'get' what you're aiming for

❖ Embrace failure, it's part of life. Reframe failure as learning so you improve next time. You only really fail if you give up

❖ Put those fears aside. Be brave and do it regardless of the fear. Nine times out of ten those fears never happen. I always ask myself 'how bad can it be' and then push on regardless

❖ Be prepared to put the work in. Nothing just lands in your lap. If something it worth having it usually takes graft, hard work, perseverance, bouncing back from adversity. I believe there's a lot of truth in the saying 'it takes 10 years to become an overnight success'

❖ Get used to be comfortably uncomfortable as that's where the growth comes, and progress is made

❖ Make sure you celebrate the wins along the way, no matter how big or small they may be. So often we're so focused on what we haven't done or achieved that we forget to give ourselves a pat on the back for all the great things you have achieved

❖ Don't have a life full or regrets. Life is too short to not follow your dreams, give it a go and be happy.

So I will leave you with these thoughts... If I can do it, you can too! You can genuinely achieve anything you want in life. In summary, it's all about setting your mindset to truly believe in yourself, being crystal-clear on what your purpose is and your reason why, plus being prepared to put the work in.

Remember you are brave, bold, and brilliant!

https://www.jeannettelinfootassociates.com

Andrew Batt (UK)

New Purposeful Living

What has led me to this point? How on earth did I reach this point in my life? As I dig deep to understand how I have arrived at this stage of my Adventure, called life, two words start to spring to mind – hope and faith. I have always 'hoped' for success in all the shapes and forms that it comes in. I always had 'faith', that I could and would achieve the success for myself. Why did I want success so badly, and so early on in my life? Because ever since I can remember, I have always had a passion to help others.

From an early age I had hardwired into my DNA the sense to protect, to assess a situation, look at things from all angles, have a watchful eye over my little brother; knowing early on that I had a sense of duty to always protect and help my younger sibling. I always put his needs ahead of my own (well unless I was winding him up for a bit of childish fun).

This sense of duty I still have today (with my brother being 41 years old), and perfectly capable of fending for himself. At just over 6-feet tall, he tends to have a presence in a room. My point here, is that this sense of duty and protection have been hardwired, unwavering, no matter what has been thrown at us both along the way, we have remained there for each other. This has never changed, no matter what, who or when this has been tested, it has been unfailing and unwavering.

This brings me back to those two words from earlier, '**hope**' and '**faith**'.

I knew that both of these would be tested, constantly during my life. We were even taught this as kids by our parents and teachers. But I always secretly hoped that my faith would not be tested like they all said. We were raised around a Christian belief system, to be kind and courteous to others, treat others how we would like to be treated ourselves, to always put others needs before our own. To be patient, as all things come to those who wait, and good things happen to good people. Our schooling involved going to Chapel three times a week whilst we were there, on a Tuesday and Thursday morning and Sunday evenings. I was on my journey of faith, I took this seriously and felt that this helped me to remain focused, on a course, and true to my own beliefs and the ones that I had been brought up around.

Just before my 8th Birthday, was the first test of my faith. Out of nowhere, my Grandfather passed away. It was a complete shock, for all of the family, but this was the first time that I ever had to deal with death. I felt like someone had ripped my heart out. And what was worse, is that I had to remain strong for my younger brother, it was my duty to protect him, and to show both of my parents that I was responsible and that they could grieve themselves, and not have to worry about the two of us.

My Grandfather was an incredible man, over 6ft tall, Ex-RAF and an Entrepreneur to boot. I have memories as early as three years old, sitting on his knee, with a colossal pink newspaper (The Financial Times) in front of both of us, whilst he would drink his tea and smoke his pipe. We would then be outside on his ride on lawnmower, or out clearing up leaves (later with my brother and cousins, we would be breaking the pains of glass in his greenhouse with footballs and cricket balls).

But he was now gone, I would never see him again, he wouldn't see me passing exams, growing up, maybe even going to university. There was a void but filled with pain, a realisation, that I would not learn more from this incredible man in my life.

After a period of time, I learnt to bury my feelings, and lock them away for safe keeping in a box. *(something that I would not recommend to anyone)*

A few years later, I decided that I should get Confirmed, I should not let the blip of my Grandfather passing away, shake my faith any further, so my Confirmation took place; I was going to continue on my path, and I would pray that my Grandmother would stay with us for years to come. I was hoping that my strength of faith would literally will this to happen, and it did. I was back on-track, but…yes there is a but!

I was struggling so much at school – I had been struggling for years – but it wasn't until I was 13 that my English teacher suspected that I was dyslexic. I took a test, and his suspicions were confirmed. There was only one thing for it, extra English lessons three times a week. He also spent extra time with me in class, pushed me harder to achieve, and constantly encouraged me (very few teachers did at the time).

He gave me renewed hope and faith at the same time. This ensured that the next couple of years I performed well in school – including all my sports – as well as spending time with my family during the holidays.

Then things started to go downhill again. My Grandmother became very ill, she struggled with her illness so much, and a few weeks before she passed away, she requested to see my brother and I. We made the trip to Cornwall – the other side of the country – during which we were both warned that she was very frail and had lost a lot of weight.

My mind was racing during the 5-hour drive – what would she look like? How was I going to cope? More importantly, I would gaze over to my brother on that journey, looking at a 12-year-old, knowing that I would need to be strong for him, just as I had been when our Grandfather passed away. My faith was yet again being tested.

Two weeks later we received the news that my Grandmother had passed away. I started to feel guilty because of my emotions. I was glad that she wasn't suffering anymore, and glad that I no longer had to remain strong for my brother and parents – a weight had been lifted from my shoulders, and I felt terrible for feeling all of these things.

At the time, the Gulf War had been televised; I was living in a world where there was so much destruction, with so many bad people in, and the good people in my life were starting to disappear. But good things happen to good people. I remember that it was around this time that I started to question everything, particularly around the Christian faith I had been using to guide me through my life so far.

Why have two people very close to me – and very good people – been taken away? I am a good person, and it seems like bad things are happening to me. My faith had been rocked to the core, then rocked some more!

I began to lose faith in everything, except one thing; the one thing that I could 100% count on, 100% of the time – myself. I would always be there for me, I would never leave me, I would never hurt me, and I would always make my own decisions, so that I could only blame me.

If I could be diagnosed with Dyslexia, and still manage to obtain a C-grade at GCSE, to then go on and achieve an English A-Level, then anything was possible. Yes, I had a considerable amount of help and support along the way, but the only person who could ultimately help, was me.

I had mostly given up on my Christian faith. But I had created a hybrid faith, one that included many of the Christian values, but I had to have faith in myself and what I was capable of. I knew I was capable of amazing things; I just didn't know what they looked like at that stage. I had a burning desire to help others and further myself.

Then is when I left for my first ski season, my right of passage, my transition from schoolboy and becoming a man. I met so many incredible people from all types of backgrounds, different upbringings and different ages. Another year and more incredible experiences. I decided that I would live everyday as if it were going to be my last, I would have plenty of time to sleep when I was dead. I was completely reckless with my own health and safety, by day I was challenging Mother Nature on my Skis or Snowboard, throwing myself off cliffs and taking on the occasional avalanche, just for kicks. By night I was partying away without a care in the world.

During this period of my life, I met someone truly incredible, she was a great friend, engaged to a superb loving and friendly man. Both were older than me in their mid-20's. I never heard her say a bad word about anyone, ever. She was kind, helpful, supportive of all of us, living in a foreign country, away from home six months at a time. There were so many fun times together, and even though we all went our separate ways after the winters, we all kept in touch; this was at a time when mobile phones were just becoming available to the masses.

Not long after, she was diagnosed with breast cancer. Initially it was a shock, but there would be no problem; she was a good person in her late 20s, fighting fit – a lifetime was ahead of her to spread even more of her goodness.

No matter how hard she fought, she ended up loosing her battle. I was devastated for her, her fiancé and her family. I remember meeting with friends before her funeral, and my thought was...'what on earth are we all doing here?' The average age of those in attendance was in the mid-twenties. This was completely wrong, I just could not process what was happening. My faith was obliterated, I only had one thing left, hope. I hoped that I would stop having to deal with this, and I hoped things would get better.

My hope kept me going, and I knew that I had to rely on my own hybrid faith. I was still here, and motivated to leave a mark on the world – to show that I could do good, help others, and do what I had always had faith that I could achieve.

I didn't know it then, but I understand it now:

- ❖ My life was starting New
- ❖ I had Purpose
- ❖ And life was for Living.

I wanted to be successful; the more success I could achieve, the more I could help others. I had to travel this painful journey to open my eyes to what I had always been traveling towards. I had to have my faith tested to breaking point and beyond, and it would be hope that carried me through on my adventure.

Do I have 'faith' now? Absolutely – faith in myself, my family and friends.

Do I have 'hope' now? Absolutely – now and forever; it carried me through everything to reach where I am today.

At the time of writing this *(early 2021)*, we are now going through an extremely difficult transition worldwide. The Covid-19 virus has spread across the world. Life as we have always known it will potentially never be the same again. We have endured periods of time of isolation, some families reunited, but struggling to live 24/7 together.

Many people have been furloughed from their jobs, children have been home-schooled, not to mention those that have had to endure the virus itself (many of whom unfortunately have not made it through).

We will make it through, I know that hope and faith in all of their forms, will carry all of us through these tough times, and all be stronger for it. We will all appreciate those that we have around us, even more. Where we can, we will make more effort to spend time together with those that we all love and cherish.

It is during this time that a few other people have put their own faith in me, and hope that I succeed in this stage of the Adventure – called Life.

I hope and have faith that I will not let them down. I know that they are there supporting me. They are my family, my parents, my brother, sister-in-law and nieces, my supportive fiancée and two future stepsons, as well as extended family and friends, coaches and mentors.

There are two friends in particular – that if it was not for both of them – I would have never realised a childhood dream of mine… to write and become an author.

They are two friends that I have known less than a couple of years, but immediately gelled with. The first is another co-author of this very book, Sharon Griffiths. Without meeting her, and forming our friendship, I would never have been introduced to the creator of Speaking From Our Hearts (Volumes 1-3), Paul D. Lowe.

Both of these friends have put, time, effort, 'faith' and 'hope' into helping me.

I will be eternally grateful to them both.

A combination of all of these struggles, experiences, meetings, a complete change of career and getting engaged, have all lead me to another stage of my life, with a renewed energy again, a new lease of life, more drive, a relentless determination to succeed and help others (I am also a big believer in Karma).

More than I have ever even contemplated up until now, they have all helped me grow towards a life of...

New Purposeful Living

Drew@NewPurposefulLiving.com

PART THREE:
HOPE FOR A BETTER LIFE

Paul D. Lowe

I Wanna Know What Love Is?

Firstly, I would like to reinforce my sincere gratitude to you the reader, for taking the time to invest in this book and also, to the global co-authors that have had the unswerving compassion to re-visit their respective life stories, in the hope that you will take something positive from the many inspiring insights and motivational messages, and as a result want to embark upon a continuous improvement journey that ultimately, enables you to give more – both to yourself and others.

From my perspective, I would also like to reinforce that motive and share how my own journey has unfolded. Yet again, in the sincere hope that your path of transformation will be one of pleasurable growth – rather than pain and suffering.

In reflecting back on the past decades and how I have come to make sense of all the pain, confusion and suffering I've experienced, I constructed 'The Hearts House'.

This is a concept that embraces all the key considerations that contribute to you feeling like you 'reside' in a very good space, one that provides a solid foundation for you to have the belief and confidence to meet all the challenges the external world has to offer, enabling you to do this because you feel more secure inside.

From a structure that is built on very solid foundations, you have the necessary insights to design your own house; one that reflects the wonderful uniqueness of you.

As an example of how to populate the house, I have 'furnished' it with my own influences…

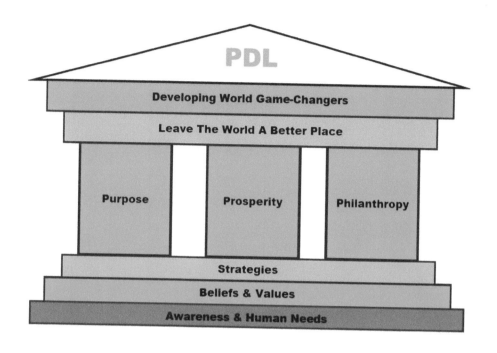

Identity: Paul D. Lowe

Mission: Developing World Game-Changers

Vision: To Leave The World A Better Place

Strategy: The Three Pillars of Life:
Purpose | Prosperity | Philanthropy

Beliefs: Your beliefs become your thoughts; which in turn become your words, actions and then, your reality

Values: Learning | Loving | Legacy

Human Needs: As human beings, we all have needs that must – and will – be met. We will do almost anything to have our needs met

Begs the question, what type of 'house' do YOU want to create?

Let Your Voice Be Heard!

We offer two ways to enable you to share your inspirational short story/ powerful message(s) with the world – either by becoming a guest on our World Game-Changers podcast, or becoming a co-author in one of our books.

In the case of our books, we are looking for people who...

❖ Have defied the odds/ overcome adversity
❖ Want to share their life-enhancing experiences, and make a difference
❖ Want to invest in being more credible experts in their industry or business(es), raise their profile and gain more visibility

Maybe you have a burning desire to become an author but writing a whole book at the moment would be a step too far – although writing a chapter (up to 3,000 words) would be achievable?

Many of our co-authors simply want to benefit from the cathartic experience of writing about their journey and sharing the lessons learnt, with a global audience.

We even offer a done-for-you service, where we record and write the chapter for you.

We make a difference by helping you make a difference – we're all about creating win-wins for everyone.

If you are interested in in becoming a co-author or a guest on a World Game-Changers podcast episode, please reach out...

ask@WorldGameChangers.org

About Paul D. Lowe

From an early age, Paul was in the vice-like clutches of the demon drink and constantly embroiled within a dark cocktail of toxic beliefs, self-hate, and destructive violence.

He has made a remarkable transformation from existing for many years in despair; to now living a really healthy, happy, and fulfilling life – spending most of his time in the sunny climes of south-east Spain.

Paul's purpose is deeply transformational:

Developing World Game-Changers...

Through his books and podcasts, he creates the space and platforms for others to be heard; Paul totally understands we all have vital messages to share, and it is part of his mission to assist people's voices to be heard – particularly our young people.

He has a long and distinguished history of heart-centred coaching & mentoring; enabling others to also enjoy a life of health, happiness, and fulfilment.

Paul has been responsible for raising very significant amounts of funds for many charities and good causes around the world;

positively impacting and inspiring thousands of children – mainly from challenging backgrounds – both within his native UK, and worldwide.

As the founder of World Game-Changers, Paul has dedicated decades of his life developing many life-empowering initiatives – contributing towards Developing World Game-Changers.

www.Paul-Lowe.com

Join The World Game-Changers Movement!

Planting The Seeds For Change

Our greatest hope is that the stories in this book inspire you to recognize that you are a world game-changer just by virtue of the fact that you live and breathe. Your presence on this planet is a reflection of your unique story and the wisdom you have cultivated through the events of your life.

You are a precious global resource.

The actions you choose to take in association with the knowledge and experience you have gathered on your journey are a demonstration of your power. We encourage you to put your power to the test and take action. The world needs you.

Humanity and all Earth inhabitants are currently bearing witness to unprecedented and historic change. As a result, we are growing in ways we could never have imagined. At the center of the chaos and upheaval is an opening, a doorway to something new, an opportunity to change, and most importantly, if we are looking closely, **hope** for a better world.

Change is inevitable. Change is the hallmark of progress. We can fight it, or we can embrace it as the golden opportunity it is. When we choose the latter, and then align ourselves with other like-minded individuals who share this perspective as well as a willingness to collaborate, we begin planting seeds that change the game in ways that honor the true, benevolent nature of the human spirit.

As seeds take root, they are nourished most fully with the love that flows through the open hearts of the collaborators. The infusion of love given freely and in abundance ensures steady and solid growth.

World Game-Changers is an organization with participants from all over the globe who have opened their hearts with the specific intent to co-create a better world. The current members have been tireless in their efforts to plant the seeds of change, quite literally in some cases!

The inaugural initiative of World Game-Changers is to plant trees – more specifically a food forest in Ghana for the benefit of the local communities. The project is well underway with 1000+ fruit and nut trees planted and growing. While it is just a start, it has been a labour of love for those with boots on the ground, as well as for those who have invested their goodwill, money, and time in the project.

You may be asking yourself as you read this, why trees? There are so many worthy causes that aim to improve the world.

We asked ourselves the same question. The answer soon became crystal-clear as we looked at what trees stand for when an opportunity to take action laid itself at our feet. Forests are Mother Nature's gift to living beings. Trees offer provisions such as sustenance, medicine, shelter, and peace to humans and animals alike. They are responsible for converting carbon dioxide to oxygen, without which, no living being would survive. They give without conditions. Trees support, sustain and promote life without prejudice.

World Game-Changers as an organization, like trees, advocates for life. We operate on the belief that all life is of great value. We believe that planting trees demonstrates beyond measure our commitment to improving life, our unfailing compassion for all living beings, our deep desire to nurture new growth, and our drive to affect productive change.

The Food Forests that we have already been responsible for planting in Ghana, is a game-changer for the people who will benefit from the bounty of the trees. It is a sign of hope that better days are imminent. We plan to spread this hope far and wide in the coming days.

Because energy and effort are amplified exponentially when two or more gather, we are asking you to hold hands with us as we seize the opportunity to take action as powerful change-makers.

Join in as World Game-Changers pool talents, hope, compassion, love, and resources, to change the game, and…

CHANGE THE WORLD!

To learn more, donate and get involved, visit our World Game-Changers Facebook group, and our website:

www.WorldGameChangers.org

CPSIA information can be obtained
at www.ICGtesting.com
Printed in the USA
BVHW020357120521
606962BV00024B/979